*What readers are saying about **Cloud***

"One of the core values at Zappos.com is to 'Embrace and Drive Change'. These new cloud services are driving the next change in the software business. The book business, on the other hand, is still pretty much the same."
Tony Hsieh, CEO, Zappos

"Whether you purchase software, develop and deliver software or are an investor in software companies, **Cloud** is a must read to understand the foundation and enduring value of the next generation in software."
Steve Singh, Chairman and CEO, Concur

"**Cloud** offers readers a concise history of the many paths to SaaS over the last seven years. By highlighting the key opportunities and issues associated with the many variants of software models, Tim prepares the reader to think through the issues and opportunities for the next seven years."
Peter Goldmacher, Managing Director, Cowen and Company

"Chou has corralled the chaos of the software industry into an engaging guide that provides insight into the current state of the industry, as well as emerging trends and changing dynamics. **Cloud** shows how winning SaaS companies are shaping the future. It's a must read for anyone interested in the anatomy of the software business."
Greg Gianforte, Chairman, Founder & CEO, RightNow Technologies

"Chou insightfully and rigorously walks through the pros and cons of software business models. A must read for any software entrepreneur or software executive."
Michael Gregoire, CEO, Taleo

"Chou's book offers a comprehensive look at what makes a software company tick and what the future of software is likely to be. Lucid and simple writing, examples and analogies that the

layperson can relate to easily, and interesting anecdotes are what set this book apart. In writing this insightful and informative book, which could well predict the future of software, Timothy Chou has made a timely and thought-provoking contribution to our knowledge about an emerging field."
Rudy Karsan, Chairman, Founder, CEO, Kenexa

"I've read a few business books that offer little new insight. Cloud is different. Not only is it well written but it contains new content about the future of the IS Business"
Walter Brenner, Professor, St. Gallen University, Switzerland

"If you are currently building, developing or managing a SaaS company, *Cloud* is a must read. Timothy has provided the best guide for success and the clearest road map for software executives to follow. His visionary yet simple recipe for building and running a SaaS company will become the must read for all executives."
Joe King, Group Vice President, Managed Services, JDA

"Timothy distills years of personal experience and an encyclopedic knowledge of the information technology industry to provide an invaluable business-oriented overview for entrepreneurs, strategists, investors, and students. Spend a few hours reading this or be prepared to spend many, many years in the field learning the same core concepts and lessons."
Sean Bandakar, Director of Programs, Executive Education, Stanford Graduate School of Business

"For those puzzled about the meaning of software as a service, *Cloud* is the book for you. We need more European companies capable of building successful challenges in the next generation of the digital economy. The book also underlines my own maxim - 'revenue is the best form of investment capital'. Read on."
Ian Taylor, Member of Parliament and former Minister for Science and Technology

"Chou shines a light on the future of software. A must read for anyone building a software-powered business."
Mark O'Neil, Chairman and CEO, DealerTrack

Cloud

Seven Clear Business Models

Timothy Chou

ISBN 978-0-6152-1359-0

Printed in the United States of America

Contents

Acknowledgements

The author would like to acknowledge numerous people in the creation of this book. These include some of the early team at Oracle that pioneered On Demand at a traditional software company: Glenn Lim, Priscilla Morgan, Don Haig, Doug McArthur, Marian Szefler, Barry Goodwin, Alberto Chacin, Mike Rocha, Lisa Arthur, Joe King, Ken Piro, Anil Thakur, and Matt Yearling. Larry Ellison's early vision in this area is not to be underestimated. He was the driving force behind not only Oracle On Demand, but also Salesforce.com and Netsuite.

In 2005, I launched a seminar class at Stanford University with the help of Claire Stager, where numerous luminaries gave their time to educate the students on their experiences. Some of these contributors have been captured explicitly and implicitly in this book, including: Charles Phillips, Brian Behlendorf, Rudy Karsan, Tom Leighton, Jonathan Schwartz, Pradeep Sindhu, Samir Aora, Evan Goldberg, Marc Benioff, Mark O'Neil, Udi Manber, Subrah Iyar, Steve Singh, Philip Rosedale, Dr. Werner

Vogels, Qianchuan Zhao, Walter Brenner, Rahul Sood, Scott Bolick, John Roberts, Maynard Webb, Dave Girourard, Erich Clementi, Greg Gianforte, Tony Hiseh, Ann Winblad, and Michael Gregoire.

Thanks to Janet Stevenson for composing the book cover. The Chinese character on the cover is the word for cloud. My mother did that calligraphy at the age of ninety. We should all be so strong. For this and more I am indebted to my parents, Mary Ann and David, whose hard work and perseverance provided me the means to realize many of my dreams. And finally thanks to my wife, Sue, and our three children, Danielle, Alexandra and Caroline, without whom the past twenty years would not have been anywhere near as meaningful or as exciting.

Introduction

Cloud computing, managed services, software as a service (SaaS), software on demand, Software+Service, platform as a service (PaaS), infrastructure as a service have all been used to describe new ways to build, deliver, and purchase software. Are they just different names for the same thing, or are they similar names for different ideas? This book is written as a primer for anyone trying to make sense of what many believe is the 3rd major wave of computing, after mainframe, and client-server computing. While it contains some aspects of technology the book is first and foremost written from a business perspective. Hence, we open with seven business models for software and use these models in the discussions throughout the remaining chapters. The book is written for anyone contemplating developing new application cloud services for internal or external usage, or for those considering moving existing applications to the cloud. In that light we introduce a five-layer cloud services stack to educate you on many of the new cloud services you can buy and not build. Finally, this book is **not** written for the experts in marketing to read the marketing section, or the VP of Operations to read the operations chapter. Instead, our mission is to deliver a holistic and balanced view useful for the CEO, general manager and all of the other team members to understand the challenges faced by the other team members.

The origins of the book can be traced to early 2002. In March of that year, the Managing Director of Oracle Germany asked to meet with me as the President of the Oracle On Demand business. During the meeting he told me he had assigned two salespeople to selling Oracle On Demand. I thought to myself that, of course, the good news was that we have two new sales people, but what I couldn't get out of my head was *"what are they saying to customers?"* I realized that the way we educate salespeople is to bring them in to the corporate campfire, tell them lots of great stories, and send them back out into the wilderness, hoping they will be able to repeat the stories.

Any student of history knows there was a massive change when Gutenberg invented the printing press. Suddenly, knowledge could stop being just campfire stories that were repeated, abused and often lost, but rather could be written down, printed and passed out to many people. So, over a long weekend, I hammered out the story I had been telling around the campfire with the intent that, perhaps during a long plane ride or over a few evenings, an Oracle salesperson or a potential customer could come to understand why moving to "software as a service" was a logical and inevitable step. That book was called *The End of Software*. Part of the book was devoted to case studies of three small private companies: Salesforce.com, RightNow Technologies, and NetSuite. None of these companies was public at that time. Salesforce.com had generated only $5M in revenue. Most people were debating why ASPs (Application Service Providers) failed and whether SaaS (Software as a Service) would be successful.

Eight years later, the world is completely different. To get an idea of how different, consider since 1999 fifteen companies, who all deliver business application cloud services, have become public companies. These fifteen include Concur (1999), Webex (2002), Kintera (2003), Salesforce.com (2004), RightNow Technologies (2004), Websidestory (2004) Kenexa (2005), Taleo (2005), DealerTrack (2005), Vocus (2005), Omniture (2006), Constant Contact (2007), Successfactors (2007), Netsuite (2007), and Opentable (2009).

Some of these companies have been acquisition targets. Webex was acquired by Cisco in March 2007 for $3.2B. Blackbaud purchased Kintera in 2008. Omniture acquired Websidestory and most recently Omniture itself was acquired by Adobe in October 2009 for $1.8B. As 2009 comes to a close the remaining eleven companies have a combined market cap of over $15B. So for those of you who wonder if companies will purchase business application software as a cloud service I think you have your answer.

Chapter 1, "Seven Vices, Seven Virtues" was originally published by the SIIA[1] (Software and Information Industry Association) and based on a talk Scott Russell invited me to give at Diamondhead Ventures in 2005. In this chapter, we outline the seven business models that encompass the entire software industry, from traditional software to open source, to outsourcing, to SaaS, to the consumer Internet. The intent is not to argue that one model is better than another, but rather to make sure, as a software business, you know which model you're trying to succeed in.

Anyone contemplating building new applications or transforming their existing applications to cloud services can today take advantage of 1000s of cloud service provided by companies large and small. We introduce the idea of a five-layer cloud service stack and dedicate Chapters 2 through Chapter 5 to covering each of the major layers. The cloud service stack is meant to further differentiate each layer of cloud services, each with a different audience. Chapter 2 begins at the application layer with application cloud services. This layer of the stack is of interest to the business users. We'll discuss all of the application

---

[1]Chou, Timothy. Seven Vices or Seven Virtues. Upgrade Magazine, June/July 2005.

areas that have benefited from being delivered as a cloud service – both horizontal and vertical. Chapter 3, "Location, Location, Location" begins at the bottom of the stack. All of the current generation of application cloud services has consumed network and datacenter cloud services. The datacenter or data center layer focuses on delivering high quality, security and reliability locations to house computers and storage. At $1,000 per square foot to build, these new data centers require a minimum outlay of $100M. While not a semiconductor fabrication line, the investment is not chicken feed. This layer is of interest to the operations team at any application, platform, or compute & storage cloud service business.

The next layer of the stack: compute and storage cloud services is discussed in Chapter 4. Pioneered by Jeff Bezos and Amazon the ability to purchase compute by the hour and storage by the month is creating an environment for a whole new range of applications. While having compute and storage available on demand is important it's likely the cloud computing war will be won by winning the developer. In Chapter 5, "Silver Bullet," we discuss horizontal and vertical platform cloud services. Horizontal services are designed to provide many of the development environments we've seen in the traditional world (e.g., Visual Studio, Ruby on Rails). However, instead of focusing only on the developer, these new platform services include much of the operational environments that were traditionally separate. Vertical platform services, while more restrictive allow the developer to leverage the data models supported by applications like salesforce.com, Netsuite and Facebook. Developing software in the newer models is not exactly the same as the traditional methods; we'll talk about how it's different and why it addresses some of the fundamental challenges we've encountered in traditional software development.

Chapter 6, "Smooth Operator," introduces perhaps the most challenging area for traditional software people, the management, and operations of the software. In this chapter, we'll address some of the major "buts", such as "...but, it's not secure," or "...but, how do we customize?" The chapter includes an interesting discussion with Lynn Reedy, who put in place the basic machinery that powers eBay.

After building the next great cloud service you'll be faced with the traditional challenge of how to market and sell the service. Chapters 7 and 8 are written for the non-sales and marketing professional. As the price points for these cloud services decrease, the challenges are even greater to find new ways to educate the buyers of your services, quickly and inexpensively. In Chapter 7 we cover some of the traditional marketing approaches as well as discuss some of the more innovative solutions. Whether you're trying to leverage your existing sales teams or build a new sales team, you'll need to figure out how to make sales & marketing a more efficient and powerful organization. All of the public application cloud service companies spend far more on sales and marketing than any other functional area. We'll hear from many experts in this area, including sales executives from WebEx, Google, Salesforce.com, and Oracle.

In the end though, any technology company requires two things to be successful: money and people. The chapter entitled "Show Me the Money" is meant for the non-finance professional and highlights some of the key financial metrics (MRR, Churn Rate, and Customer Lifetime Value) that are important to running a subscription business. Finally, Chapter 10, "People Needing People," may be at the end of the book, but we all should remember that every software business is a people business. Having a solid culture, stage-appropriate leadership and the right specialist in the right organizational structure are as key as picking the right development methodology or sales compensation structure.

I hope this book will serve to inform you, whether you're in R&D, sales, channel management, or QA. The challenge of moving to software as a service in the cloud is not simply a shift from C++ to Java. The challenge forces all parts of our organizations, from sales to operations to finance, to rethink the accepted ways of designing, selling, and delivering software.

Finally we believe the campfire stories and lessons in *Cloud* apply to all businesses. As long time venture capitalist Ann Winblad said recently, "This is one thing that's really changing in the marketplace. Everybody is a software company, not just the companies in the software industry."

1

SEVEN VICES, SEVEN VIRTUES

In the 6th century, Pope Gregory the Great, one of only two Popes to be given the title, "the Great", defined the Seven Deadly Sins, or as they are sometimes called, the Seven Deadly Vices. These were: Pride, Envy, Gluttony, Lust, Anger, Greed and Sloth. Not only did Pope Gregory define the seven sins to avoid, he also included a balancing set of values, the Seven Virtues: Faith, Hope, Charity, Fortitude, Justice, Prudence and Temperance. Many would agree that managing a software company requires a little of both.

CLOUD

Today, as the software industry undergoes a major transformation to a cloud computing model, it's important to understand the seven potential business models before deciding if they are a Vice or a Virtue. You will hear some say, "We can't move to a SaaS model, the sales guys will never be able to sell it," while others will talk endlessly about the virtues of the model and how, "It'll be great to not have to wonder if this quarter we'll close that big deal at midnight on December 31." As you'll see some companies operate in only one model; others have products that operate in multiple models.

The seven business models are complete and include every company that makes money from their software. There are successful companies in each of the models. The models are oriented around application software and we'll start from the traditional world of business software.

	1 Traditional	2 Open Source	3 Outsourcing	4 Hybrid	5 Hybrid+	6 SaaS	7 Web
Software	$4,000/user (one time)	$0 (one time)	$4000/user (one time)	$4,000/user (one time)	$300/user/ month	<$100/user/ month	Ads Transactions Embeded (<$10/user, month)
Support	$800/user/ year	$1,600/user (one time)	$800/user/year	$800/user/year			
Service			Bid <$1,300/ user/month	$150/user/ month			
			@H @C	@H @C	@H @C		

Figure 1.1 Seven Business Models

Model One: Traditional

This is the traditional software business model, mastered by many companies, including Oracle and SAP. The software is licensed in perpetuity with a one-time price, in our example, of $4,000 per user. Subsequently, the customer is charged some percentage; say 20 percent, for the update/upgrade rights as well as maintenance, sometimes referred to as the software support fee. In our case study, this translates to about $65 per user per month, or around $800 per user per year. Many would point out that even traditional software companies have large subscription businesses. In fact in late 2009, Oracle's maintenance business is over $12B annually.

The business that bought the software then buys hardware, and hires or redeploys people to manage the software. It's here that the spending really goes up. The Gartner Group has estimated that the end user can spend up to four times the cost of their software license per year to manage these applications. This cost multiplier is not limited to complex business software. Why does it cost so much?

Amy Konary, at International Data Corporation (IDC), and one of the earliest industry analysts to follow the change to software delivered as a service, cites five major areas that cost companies millions of dollars annually. "CIOs and their departments really focus on five key aspects of the management and maintenance of their computer and software systems: availability, performance, security, problems, and change management." The implications of this are substantial. First, CIOs' budgets are dominated by spending on managing software, leaving little money on the table for new programs and projects. In our example, while the purchase price of the software may be $4,000 per user, the customer will end up spending $1,300 per user **per month** just to manage that software.

Some software companies also provide additional support services, so called premium support, which often conflict with their partners or internal consulting groups who also provide value added services to help the customer service the software. A Model One business is good since, with the large up-front purchase of the software, sales and marketing expense, which typically can run thirty to forty percent of revenue, can be funded. At a well-run Model One business, you'll see license revenue breaking even, and all of the profit realized from software support. Software support or maintenance is mostly limited to break-fix; access to a Web site of usage information and upgrades. It is, of course, in the software company's interest to move customers forward on new releases so as to not incur expense in supporting multiple releases of the software. In the early stages of any software company, this is mutually beneficial, as the customer needs and wants future functionality and, in many ways, that's why the consumer chooses to buy versus build. WebEx founder Subrah Iyar, lecturing at Stanford in 2006, said "I would much rather have built a software business on the traditional model—it's a much better business model for the software company."

Model Two: Open Source

The free software movement began in the late 80s. By 1998, a group of programmers came up with open source as a replacement for free software, creating the Open Source Initiative (OSI) to promote the new term. Under the name "open source," an in-flux of for-profit dollars has changed the landscape of free software remarkably. Most major free software projects now have corporate backing of one form or another, and many of these companies have become quite adept at working with the community that participates in the projects, and the users who report bugs and suggest new features.

In May 2005, IBM made an acquisition of Gluecode Software, a privately held company specializing in integration software based in El Segundo, CA. The purchase price was estimated at $100M. A year later, in June 2006, Red Hat, the world's best-known Linux distributor, announced the acquisition of JBoss for a reported $420M. In early 2008 Sun Microsystems surprised everyone with their $1B acquisition of MySQL.

All of this has not been lost on the investment community. Over the past many years, at least $500M has been invested in a variety of open source software companies. Why? The open source model (much like Google) has reduced the entry cost to "try it" to zero. MySQL estimates there have been 100 million installations and over 60 thousand downloads per day. JasperSoft estimates there have been nearly two million downloads and over 20 thousand corporate deployments in 200+ countries of their Jasper Reports. John Roberts, the founder of SugarCRM has shown a Google map with the heartbeat from hundreds of computers in Europe running SugarCRM software—and SugarCRM has no sales force in Europe.

While having people download, install, and potentially use your software is far better than having them download a brochure, open source software companies have struggled with the business model. Support and maintenance, which has been the lifeblood of Model One software companies, has been difficult to monetize. Traditional bronze, silver, and gold support has also been difficult to sell, since there has been little value-add other than changing the hours you will answer the phone and how quickly you'll respond to a request. Some open source companies are experimenting with providing both appliances and an on-demand solution as a way of providing a higher degree of service than traditional software support. Some are providing additional functionality in a paid-for subscription service not available in their free version. Unfortunately, other than Red Hat with their Red Hat Network, revenue has been elusive. But with lots of money and smart people, it may not be for long.

Model Three: Outsourcing.

Recognizing that the cost to manage software systems is much larger than the purchase price of the software, companies have emerged who are eager to take on the challenge. EDS (purchased by HP) and IBM Global Services have each built large, multi-billion dollar businesses outsourcing the management of the software and systems. In Model Three software is still licensed from the software company on a perpetual basis; support fees are still paid, but now the Model Three business will take on the management of that software for less than the $1,300 per user per month the customer would be spending. Outsourcers can manage the software either at the client's site or at their own locations. As much of the cost of the software management is buried in the cost of people, a new group of companies, such as Infosys, have emerged, using offshore resources in India to lower the overall cost. Of course today every Model Three business is leveraging a global pool of talent whether in India, China or Eastern Europe.

Model Three can grow big companies and high value companies. EDS at the time it was acquired was over $20B in revenue. IBM Global Services generates over 50 percent of IBM's revenue, which, in 2007, was $50B. Tiny Infosys with over $3B in revenue has traded at more than eight times revenue, a multiple most software companies would be glad to have. These companies continue to grow and take on higher value functions, including entire business processes. ADP is probably the granddaddy of this business model.

While Model Three is good, there are two key challenges. First, over time, massive differences in labor rates are not sustainable. Second, the dependence of system availability on people, with the inherent risk of human error, is also not sustainable. IBM has recognized that they could grow their Global Services business by a factor of two, bringing them to over $100B in revenue. While the opportunity is there, they would erode their margins. Fortunately, or unfortunately, they are already in the low cost countries—Brazil, Russia, India, and China—so unless there are highly skilled resources in Antarctica waiting to be discovered, IBM will need to invest in technology. Jim Spohrer founded an initiative inside IBM called Service Science. Spohrer has said, "One grand research challenge for us is how to scale up services and how to invest to get year-over-year improvements." Computer science has benefited from Moore's Law (where the capabilities of computer chips double about every 18 months). Could a Moore's Law of service science be possible?

Model Four: Hybrid.

For most traditional software companies, Model Four, the Hybrid model, represents a bridge from Model One to Model Six: This business model attempts to leverage what an existing software company already has: products, distribution channel, and an installed base. In Model Four the traditional licensing model is retained. In our example, that means the software is still licensed for $4,000 per user with a support fee of 20 percent or $65 per user per month. The big difference in Model Four is to give the purchaser the choice of having the software company service their own software. This is the model Oracle pursued beginning in 1999 and resulted in the fastest growing business inside of Oracle in 2004. Customers ranged from middle market to Fortune 500 companies and spanned the range of applications from financials to HR, manufacturing, and CRM and supply chain. From the consumer's perspective, the choice was between servicing the software themselves for around $1,300 per user per month, having a Model Three business provide the service for less than $1,300, or having Oracle service their own software for $150 a month. We'll come back to answer the question as to why was it so inexpensive, but first let's make sure you're clear on the model.

In Model Four, the purchase of the software and support remain the same. What's new is the customer is given an option to have the availability, security, performance, and changes managed for an additional fee. With Oracle On Demand, the customer had a one year contract that could be cancelled with 30-days notice, and rather than have a complex Service Level Agreement (SLA), there was a "Nordstrom's guarantee". Oracle guaranteed if for any reason the customer were unhappy with the service, there would be a 20 percent rebate in that month, no questions asked. It's important to note this decision enabled revenue to be recognized on a monthly basis.

Unlike some lighter weight business processes (e.g., email, sales force tracking, recruiting) customers of Oracle applications implemented much heavier weight processes (e.g., process or discrete manufacturing). As a result, there needed to be flexibility to customize and integrate the applications. An innovation was provided called CEMLIs, which isolated changes that were made for one customer, which could be separately priced and give a customer the choice of how much they valued their customizations. There will be more on this in a later section.

Additionally, customers were also given the flexibility to choose where the computers would be located—either at an Oracle owned data center or at a location of their choice. There will be more on this later as well. Figure 1.1 illustrates this flexibility by using the symbols of @H (for at home) meaning a data center owned by the business providing the service. @C (for at customer) means a site the customer owns.

Model Four also allowed customers to choose when changes would be made to the application and when upgrades to major releases would occur. While there was a great deal of flexibility versus what you will find in either Model Six or Model Seven, there was also a great degree of standardization. This started from the hardware and moved up to the disaster recovery process. For example, all applications were run on a Linux multi-tier grid, disks were network attached versus SAN attached; and, while you could choose when upgrades happened, they always followed the same process.

Which gets us back to—how was it possible to offer the service at significantly lower prices than a traditional outsourcer? Could this business be operated at "product level" margins? The quick answer is, yes, product level margins could be achieved because of a high degree of standardization. Standardization allows for specialization. Specialization allows for repetition, the key to quality and skill in any area, whether managing computers or doing heart surgery. With repetition based on specialization, ultimately computers could be put to work automating the key business processes in the business of servicing software. A simple example is upgrades. Oracle On Demand upgrades were done hundreds of times in a year by specialized teams, and increasing parts of the upgrade process were automated. Automation ultimately results in both lower cost and higher quality service. By the way, this principle is followed in spades by Model Six and Seven businesses.

The advantage of this model is that the software does not have to be re-engineered. And, from a sales perspective, since the traditional license model is preserved, you can use your existing sales channel. The model is **not** cannibalistic. In fact, since the sales teams were compensated not only on the sale of the license but also the first year of the service, the average selling price nearly doubled for on-demand applications. In addition, the ability to offer a complete solution from one vendor was often a significant competitive advantage against traditional software companies who had to go to partners for the solution.

Finally, by having a model that split the software license from the service, the entire installed base of customers who had already bought the software was open for business. There were many situations where there were no traditional software sales persons assigned to customer accounts that had bought a lot of software, because they had bought all the software they could eat—an interesting paradox.

Of course, any model is not without its downsides. Alternate channels of software distribution do not welcome Model Four. They have made a living selling "boxes and bodies" and see the vendors' entry into this space as competitive. The second downside is the model can only take you so far from a cost perspective. The cost, not price, of providing this service is in the neighborhood of $50 per user per month, which compares favorably with doing it yourself or having an outsourcer provide the service, which is probably closer to $500 per user per month. But if someone could provide 80 percent of the function of your product at $5 per user per month, then you would no longer stay in Model Four. This of course is the story of Siebel and Salesforce.com. More on that later.

Model Five: Hybrid+

Many people see the SaaS model as a change in the way software is purchased—in particular, the elimination of the upfront license fee. While Model Four allows for the delivery model to change, it is easy to see you are not far from moving the business model as well. In our example, if one were to assume a 36-month time to pay off the $4,000 per user license fee, this would equate to $110 per user per month, adding the $65 per user per month for support and the $150 to manage the software results in an "all in" price of $325 per user per month. Of course, the revenue recognized in the first year is less than in Model One, but midstream in the second year this begins to change. By the third year, this model is resulting in much larger revenue stream than was true in the traditional model. The choice of moving from Model Four to Model Five is strictly a business choice, not a technology choice.

Callidus Software, a provider of sales performance management solutions, has adopted this business model. Rather than split the license from the service as we have seen in Model Four, they are providing one price for the entire service. Since Leslie Stretch became CEO in December 2006 the company's subscription revenue as a percentage of total revenue has nearly doubled, representing nearly 40% of total revenue.

Model Six: Software as a Service

As we discussed briefly in Model Four, the cost to manage the software can be driven down through standardization, repetition, and automation, but there is a floor. If you get to start from scratch and engineer an application for delivery as a service (and only a service) the cost structures drop by another order of magnitude. Most, if not all, of the new business software companies started in the late 90s have adopted this model. As a business model, even MMORPG (Massively Multi-player Online Role Playing Games) like *World of Warcraft* have adopted Model Six.

Software engineered for Model Six will have dramatically lower cost structures than software as a service offered by traditional software companies. Siebel had to face the direct challenge of Salesforce.com, UpShot and others. While these new companies' offerings had far less functionality, the cost and, as we'll see, simplicity of purpose allowed them to compete very effectively.

Model Six is not without its challenges. While it is clearly a better model for the consumer of the software, one can debate whether it's a better model for the software company. Unfortunately, rather than being able to close million-dollar deals for software licenses in Model One, and being able to plow that cash back into sales and marketing, companies in Model Six have to find a way to finance the early acquisition of customers. This has typically been done in the private and public markets. If you analyze Salesforce.com, WebEx, and Concur you will find it took somewhere between $50M and $100M to establish the distribution channels required to achieve their meteoric growth.

Furthermore, as in Model Four and Five, the existing channels, such as the Microsoft channel, are at best ambivalent to the Model Six players. With no easy distribution channel, many companies in Model Six reach $10M in revenue and have no ability to grow larger.

Model Seven: Internet

Model Seven encompasses all of the companies in the consumer Internet. Amazon, Facebook, Google, Yahoo and eBay are all software companies. Model Seven is distinctive in a few ways. First, these companies have chosen unique and often indirect ways to monetize their intellectual property, the software. Whether it is eBay charging by transaction, Google by the ad, or Zappos by embedding it in the sales transaction, each of the companies in Model Seven has adopted business models that are asymmetric. Asymmetric business models mean that the user of the software is not directly paying for the usage of the software. We all use Google for free; it's the advertisers that are paying for it. Of course that does not mean Model Seven companies have no cost of sales and marketing. You only need to look at eBay's or Google's financials to realize that there is a healthy spend on sales and marketing.

The second big difference is that each of these solutions is highly specialized. You don't buy books, auction cars or find your perfect mate on Google. Google, eBay, and Amazon.com have all been very focused on a single function. Why? Again, it comes to cost. In the traditional world, if I built some interesting software in Sydney, Australia, and I wanted to expand to Melbourne, I had to hire a sales/support engineer and a salesperson. My cost of distribution meant that I needed to extract the greatest degree of value out of each of my customers. That model resulted in the classical software company "going horizontal"—meaning they began to offer more and more parts of the solution, all the time promising full integration, so no new company could get in the door. This has led to massive suites of applications. Unfortunately, these applications tend to be complex, difficult to install, and difficult to integrate—no one needs to spend much time comparing a traditional enterprise application to consumer Internet applications to see the difference. Of course, this all shows up in the speed of adoption. The simplicity of the Google interface begged for millions, if not billions, of people to adopt—clearly not possible if the application tried to do everything.

Economics of Software

I started teaching a seminar class at Stanford (CS309A) on software as a service in 2005, and one thing I spend a lot of time on is the economics of software, because most people have never thought much about it. If you went to work for Dell you'd be well educated on the cost-or economics-of hardware, but how do we determine the cost of software? I'm not talking about the price of the software, but the cost. Some will say the cost of software is the cost of the CD or the manual, but, in fact, the cost of software is much, much more. I'm going to use eBay to help explain how the cost of traditional software differs from that of delivering software from the cloud.

Let's assume ten years ago we wanted to start a company building auctioning software. We would have hired a bunch of smart programmers. They'd have just gotten out their C++ compilers and ultimately created an auction product. But the first question the CEO would have asked would be, "Okay, how do we get it to anybody?" Some smart VP of Sales and Marketing would have said, "No problem, boss. I got the plan. Let's put it in the Sunday paper," so a million CDs would go out in the Sunday paper. What would have happened on Monday morning? My guess is the 1-800 number would be ringing with calls: "Hey, wait a minute. This really ruined my Windows 95 configuration, and my ShockWave DLL doesn't run anymore." "No problem," we would say, "We're software guys, and we can solve this." Then we'd hire a support team, set up a help desk, and so on.

A few months or years later, some bright product manager would show up and say, "Hey, boss, got a really great idea. I got a new feature I want everybody to see. It's called 'Buy It Now.' Let's put it in the next release." No problem, right? We would insert the CD in the next Sunday paper. Monday morning would arrive and the first phone call would start with "My Linux server just fell over after I installed your software." No problem. We'll hire a bunch more support guys, we'll move them to India. Problem solved.

Now, all of us in the traditional software business know how to do this. We've been doing this since the beginning of software. The problem is economic. What would have been the cost of that scenario? It would have been enormous. There is no way eBay could possibly have existed under this software cost model. The cost for delivering the software, distributing it, and managing it would have been so prohibitive eBay would have had to charge hundreds of dollars for every auction. While you could have built a small auctioning software business, no way you would have been a multi-billion dollar business.

If you think about what has transformed the entire hardware industry, it has been a relentless pursuit of taking cost down by an order of magnitude every decade. It has completely transformed the hardware business. In the beginning of the 80s, hardware companies like Digital Equipment Corporation, Burroughs, and Data General dominated the scene and companies like Intel were dismissed as not delivering real computers. "Well, that microprocessor stuff is cool, but it's never going to amount to much." We all know the end of that story.

So what do the real numbers look like? If you take enterprise software-say from SAP or Oracle-and you deliver it as an on-demand service, you're going to do really well if the cost (not price) is $50 per user per month. By the way, you're going to have to standardize the hell out of everything, so you'd do really well to get it out there at $50. Now remember, chances are, if the customer is running this software in house, it's costing them closer to $1000 per user per month, so even if SAP or Oracle charges $150, it's significantly lower than having each and every customer of the software solve the problems uniquely.

Now, if you become a student of Salesforce.com, and analyze their cost (the cost of delivering the software), guess what that number is?-about $7 per user per month. That's impressive. Remember, of course, this is for a fixed set of functions, and if you want to control when you upgrade, forget about it. But that's not the end of our story. If you go down 101 to Mountain View and estimate what it costs Google to deliver their service, you'll come away with a number closer to $0.70 per user per month. Bottom line: anyone in the software business needs to become a student of the economics of software.

Summary

While it may not be clear to you which model to choose, one thing *is* clear—the traditional software model is ending. With increased competition and the dynamics of the open source movement, the days of million-dollar software licenses are clearly over. And, with increased pressure on top line growth without fundamentally altering the cost structure of software companies, we will be at the end of software.

You will have many choices. You can choose to use Model One and Model Four, which is what Oracle did. You can choose to move completely to Model Six, which is what Concur did. You can choose to start out a new business in Model Six, which is what Salesforce.com did. You can choose to acquire Model Six companies, and have some of your product line in Model One, some in Model Four and some in Model Six, which is what Blackbaud did.

Whatever you choose to do you'll need to think about how the choices affect the entire company; since unlike the change to client-server, this shift is much more than technology. In the next chapter we'll drill down a little more into some of the application areas and companies that have been successful in delivering their applications as a cloud service.

2

APPLICATION CLOUD SERVICES

It's far easier to talk about business models and the new cloud computing services from the point of view of an application any of us would use in a business setting. In this chapter we're going to introduce you to a variety of both horizontal (everyone can use) and vertical (specialized to a particular industry) applications. We're going to focus only on application areas, which have companies who have succeeded in bringing their companies into the public market.

I was having lunch in early 2007 with an old friend Tom Kucharvy. He said, "You know, Tim, you've been talking a lot about this software as a service, software on demand thing. Now when is this going to really happen?" His question got me to thinking, so I did a little homework. I went back to 1999 and looked up nine (at the time) of the business application software companies, who all deliver their software as a service, and who all have gone public since 1999. Since then some of them have been acquired (Webex, Kintera, Websidestory, Omniture), but the remaining eleven have a combined market capitalization of over $15B, so it's safe to say, "It's happened!" So let's start our discussion of what areas have seen success.

Collaboration

Of all of the application areas, perhaps the simplest (from a business point of view) is collaboration. The way you use email vs. your friend at another company is not significantly different. As a result some of the more successful application cloud service companies have started out in collaboration. Collaborative software or groupware includes features such as email, calendaring, conferencing, instant messaging, wikis and simple project management. The granddaddy of all collaborative software, Microsoft, of course delivers email (Hotmail) but more recently introduced Exchange Online and SharePoint Online. Microsoft Office chief Chris Capossela predicts[2] that 50% of

---

[2] Fast Company, October 28, 2008.

Exchange mailboxes will be online within five years. They might be able to achieve this, as there are reports of large companies, including Coca-Cola and Nokia, using their collaboration cloud offerings.

This, of course, is a major battleground area. Google has brought its considerable resources to bear by introducing Google Apps which includes mail, calendaring, and the ability to collaborate around spreadsheets, presentations and text documents. IBM, not to be left behind has introduced Lotus Live and continues to innovate in this area. But perhaps the company that did the most to prove that collaborative application cloud services could be a high growth standalone business is Webex.

Webex Story

Min Zhu and Subrah Iyar founded WebEx in late 1996 as a re-start of another company called FutureLabs. FutureLabs focused on providing software-client and client-server solutions for data conferencing. In 1995, FutureLabs was acquired by Quarterdeck. It was then that Subrah, who was responsible for Quarterdeck's acquisition of FutureLabs, met FutureLabs founder Min. Within a year of the acquisition, Microsoft introduced NetMeeting and ended Quarterdeck's interest in the space. Fortunately, Iyar and Min saw the potential of continuing as a service provider, so they launched WebEx.

Although they started WebEx in 1996, it took Subrah and Min until 1999 to actually launch the service. During 1997 and 1998, they spent a lot of time working with customers such as Charles Schwab and StrataCom, which, ironically, was also purchased by Cisco. In 1999, WebEx generated about $2.5 million in revenue with about 400 customers; by 2000, revenues were $25 million, and the rest, as they say, is history. WebEx went public in January 2002. By their 10th anniversary, they were generating nearly $500M. With over two million registered users and over 85,000 meetings per day around the globe, Webex continues to deliver one of the largest application cloud services in use today.

While collaboration is the modern day telephone, perhaps the first business software any company purchases is a financial application. Whether an Excel spreadsheet, Intuit QuickBooks, Microsoft Dynamics, Oracle Financials or SAP every company large or small needs a financial application.

Financial Applications

Financial applications record and process accounting transactions within functional modules such as accounts payable, accounts receivable and payroll. Financial applications can help provide cash & treasury management, financial control and reporting, financial analytics, governance, procure-to-pay, and travel & expense management. The most complex and expensive business accounting software is frequently part of an extensive suite of software often known as enterprise resource planning (ERP) software.

This area has not been easy to penetrate for application cloud service companies, perhaps for two reasons. First, almost every company has a financial application and second, that application generally has few users. That being said two companies have been quite successful in this area. Concur made an initial public offering in 1999 and has grown a large business specializing in travel and expense management. Netsuite, who made a public offering in 2007, has mirrored the "suite-approach" pioneered by Oracle and SAP and instead focused on the middle market.

Concur Story

While Oracle was one of the leaders in moving from a traditional model to software delivered as a service, few examples compare with Concur. Concur began life as a traditional software company, but in June 2000, chairman and CEO Steve Singh made a bold decision to reinvent the whole company and make the transition to delivering their expense management software as a service. This was a major challenge, particularly since they were a public company. The stock sank to below $1 a share, and the number of employees went from 700 to 300. By the end of the transformation, nearly the entire senior management team was replaced. Of course if you were smart enough to purchase the stock at the low point your returns would be over 40x today.

Since those lean years early in this decade, Concur has steadily held to its mission. By the end of 2006, Concur had over 4,000 clients, with seven of the world's ten largest companies using their services to help them manage the corporate travel and expense process. Their customers include Vivek Ahuja, Global Operating Manager at Agilent, a global measurement equipment company; Courtney McCoy, Senior Business Systems Analyst at Cummins, Inc., a leader in diesel engine technology and Gloria Brown, A/P & Payroll Supervisor at Stryker Medical, a $5B+ medical technology company. While some question whether such a transition from a Model One provider to a leading Model Six service provider would be possible in the public markets today, few can debate the success of the bold decisions that Steve Singh and Concur made.

Netsuite Story

NetSuite is a leading provider of integrated online software that allows SMBs to manage their entire business in a single application. Evan Goldberg, Dave Lipscomb, Bill Ford, and Chris Blum founded the company under the name NetLedger in October 1998, with financing from Larry Ellison. Today, Evan Goldberg is Chairman of the Board and Zach Nelson is the company's CEO. The company launched its first online financial application targeting small businesses in 1999. With this foundation, the company broadened the application to manage both back-office and front-office sales, support and marketing. The company changed its name in September 2003 from NetLedger to NetSuite and made a successful IPO in December of 2007.

Netsuite's customers include Todd Spartz, CFO, Nomis Solutions, a price optimization solution for the financial services industry; Everette Phillips, President and CEO of China Manufacturing Network and David Stover, CFO of Asahi Kasei Spandex America. Asahi Kasei, located in Charleston, S.C., is a subsidiary of Tokyo-based Asahi Kasei Fibers Corp., a Tokyo-based manufacturer of polyelastane filament fibers used mainly in textiles. You might find it hard to believe but they replaced their SAP R/3 with Netsuite in 2008.

Human Resource Applications

Along with financial applications, human resource (HR) applications were an early example of widely adopted business applications. Peoplesoft, is perhaps the best known company specializing in HR software. It was founded in 1987 and ultimately acquired by Oracle for $10B in 2004. Human resource applications are built to assess, acquire, develop, and align a businesses workforce. Beginning with tracking of resumes of prospective employees to keeping record of employees' compensation & benefits, performance appraisals, HR software tracks the lifecycle of many companies most valuable asset: their people.

It turns out this has also been a good area for application cloud service companies including three companies that have made initial public offerings in the past five years – Kenexa in June 2005, Taleo in October of 2005 and Successfactors in 2007.

Kenexa Story

While Salesforce.com and WebEx started out knowing what they wanted to be, Kenexa took the long way home. Kenexa is the oldest of the group, having been founded by Rudy Karsan in 1987. Kenexa began operations in 1987 not as a software company, but as a recruiting firm. Over the past 20+ years, Kenexa has bought and sold over twenty businesses. Through these acquisitions, Kenexa has grown its business to over $160M in revenue in 2009. Today, Kenexa is a provider of software: proprietary content, services and process outsourcing that enable organizations to more effectively recruit and retain employees. But Kenexa's path has not been without its challenges. At a lecture at Stanford University, Karsan talked about a day in 1991 when he had mortgaged his house, maxed out his credit cards, and was three months late in the office rental payments. On a certain Friday, the landlord had told him the sheriff would be coming on Monday to evict them. The good news was that the company had sold a $40,000 contract to a large insurance company. Typically, the customer would have waited to the last day to pay, but for some reason the checked arrived early, on that Friday. Karsan took the check, drove from Philadelphia to New York City, cashed the check at the issuing bank, and was ready on Monday morning with his rent payment. His message to the students was, you might be as hard working and as smart as the next group, but, in the end, success is based on a lot of luck. This was his lucky story.

Taleo Story

Taleo traces its beginnings to 1996, when founder Martin Ouellet created Viasite, which would become the most successful job board in Canada. Following on that success, Ouellet founded Recruitsoft in 1998 and joined forces with Louis Tetu, who had a background in supply chain management. Tetu understood by leveraging the power and connectivity of the Internet, one could deliver a talent supply chain management solution that provided the same bottom-line and process improvement benefits to large enterprises that supply chain management had brought to manufacturing.

Taleo joined fellow application cloud service companies DealerTrack, Kenexa and Vocus in going public in 2005. By late 2007, Taleo had over 12 hundred customers, one million users, and had tracked over 66 million candidates. Taleo's software is used by Fortune 500 companies as well as smaller companies to match all sources of talent—be they professional and hourly candidates, agency referrals, campus recruits, contingent workers, or existing employees—to all positions, whether it is centralized, decentralized, or multinational. Some

33

of Taleo's customers include Randy Goldberg, VP of Recruiting at Hyatt Hotels & Resorts, which manages over 100,000 rooms in over 40 countries; Christoph Thoma, Head of HR at Roche, a global healthcare company employing over 75,000 people worldwide; and Bruce Hatz, Global Staffing Director at Applied Materials, an $8B+ provider of semiconductor fabrication equipment.

CEO Michael Gregoire is uniquely qualified to see the similarities and differences between traditional and application cloud service companies, as he was an Executive Vice President at PeopleSoft before joining Taleo. He sees the challenges of the traditional software business as being interlocked with the technology. Meaning that, today, if a traditional software company wants to deliver any significant function, there must be a schema change. With a schema change comes an upgrade, and, given the often-high degree of customization most customers apply, the cost for the upgrade becomes prohibitive. Hence, the business can't move forward since the technology can't move forward. Mike's lecture at Stanford in 2007 was entitled: "Does Business Evolution Drive Technical Innovation or Does Technical Innovation Drive Business Evolution?" He ended the talk by saying, "Yes!"

Successfactors Story

Sometimes you can tell a company is different when you walk in the door. A few years back I went to the SuccessFactors headquarters to meet with Lars Dalgaard, founder and CEO. The office had no cubicles, no separate offices, and furniture that had been specially designed to reinforce that each individual was part of a team. Many companies are born on the personal experiences and frustrations of their founder. Successfactors is no different. On graduation Lars went to work for Novartis, a large pharmaceutical company based in Switzerland. In short order he was headhunted by Unilever. When he went to the VP of HR to inform him of his decision the VP got a key out of his pocket, opened a closet and pulled out a huge three ring binder, skimmed through it, and then pulled out all a set of org charts and said, "See, here you are. You are going to be running Portugal in two years!"

Lars said: "What? What are you talking about?" The VP came back and said, "Well, that's not the only one. I also have you in Germany, but that is a lower job. I also have you ..." and he started going through more and more org charts. All Lars could think was "Is this is how they manage careers?"

Out of that epiphany he founded Successfactors in 2001. In 2007 they made a successful initial public offering, and in 2008 placed number 133 on Deloitte's 2008 Technology Fast 500. Their solution is deployed to over four million end users in over 30 languages. Their customers are as small as Jay Greenstein, owner of the Sport and Spine Rehab centers based in Virginia and as large as Brenda Leadley, a VP of global human resources for Allianz Group. Allianz Group was founded in 1890, and is one of the leading global services providers in insurance, banking and asset management with more than 180,000 employees worldwide.

CRM for Marketing

Customer Relationship Management (CRM) is a company-wide business strategy designed to reduce costs and increase profitability by managing a customer lifecycle from initial marketing, to closing the sale, servicing the customer and ultimately delivering more products and service to the same customer. CRM's goal is to bring together information from all data sources within an organization (and where appropriate, from outside the organization) to give one view of the customer. The goal is to allow customer-facing employees in sales, customer support, and marketing to make quick, informed decisions.

This area has been very fruitful for application cloud service providers. In the next three sections we'll divide up CRM into CRM for marketing, sales and finally service. CRM for marketing includes solutions to track PR effectiveness, email marketing, web analytics and soon new innovations in social media marketing. If the software can increase the number of qualified leads for sales then it's CRM for marketing. This group includes products from Vocus, Omniture and Constant Contact.

Vocus Story

Vocus was co-founded by Rick Rudman and Bob Lentz in 1992. The company, based in Lanham, Maryland, went public in December 2005 and provides on-demand, Web-based software for public relations. Their platform monitors news, sends out press releases, and helps communicate with the media and the public. Today they have over 2000 active customers representing organizations of all sizes across a wide variety of industries.

As a part of their solution, Vocus provides a proprietary information database of over 800,000 journalists, analysts, media outlets, and publicity opportunities. Their database contains information about the media, including in-depth journalist profiles, contact schedules, podcast interviews, pitching preferences, and other relevant information compiled by its dedicated media research team. The Vocus database is integrated with a suite of on-demand modules that, together, address the communications life cycle, from identifying key contacts, to distributing information, to closing the loop with digitized feedback and management analytics.

Vocus's application is used by a wide variety of organizations. After a successful career in television news at ABC, Christine Nyirjesy Bragale, joined Goodwill Industries International, one of the largest nonprofit organization in North America, as international spokesperson and Director of Media Relations. When she joined, all media relationships were tracked and managed in a notebook (no, not a computer—a real notebook). By replacing the notebook with Vocus they are able to not only access records of interactions with journalist but also be able to measure the results of news coverage. For a business that is over $2B in revenue that's no small step.

Omniture Story

Josh James and John Pestana met as undergraduates at a computer science class at Brigham Young University. They focused their first business on Web design, developer's tools, and gathering Web visitor data primarily for small businesses.

While it was a good business the cancellation rate for these small businesses was so high they had to constantly run to stay in place. Luckily, some large enterprise customers saw the value of their software and it didn't take them long to shift their focus to providing Web analytics solutions for those larger customers. Reflecting the new business focus, the company was renamed Omniture in 1998. Omniture is derived from the words "omniscient" and "future."

Josh recalls the early days when they were offering software as a service, before people even knew what to call it. "In the early days, we had to fight through numerous issues, like security, redundancy, and availability. We decided the best thing to do was to go after the larger companies and then use them as references."

Today, Omniture is used in a wide variety of applications. Overstock.com was losing customers in the checkout process. Using Omniture's SiteCatalyst software, they refined their checkout process from seven down to three Web pages, resulting in a 70 percent increase in conversion rates. In another application, Novell uses Omniture SiteCatalyst on their corporate intranet to track the use of applications, static Web pages, and dynamic Web pages. Based on this data, Novell can better expose pages, remove them, or adjust resources so that they don't have to spend money on pages or applications that are not being accessed.

More recently, Omniture acquired Visual Sciences, which had themselves, acquired WebSideStory and now finds itself as one of the gorillas in Web analytics. Josh loves the subscription business model, which he likens to a freight train. Since your competitors cannot see the bookings, only the revenue, it seems as if the business is growing slowly at first. But, "just like a freight train, by the time you hear it, it's rocketing past you— and there is no way to catch up!"

Constant Contact Story

Constant Contact, Inc. was incorporated as Roving Software in 1995. The company had just seven employees and a handful of clients when Gail Goodman took the reins in 1999. Goodman raised more than $20M in her first year and launched the company's first product: a permission-based email tool. Gail's advice to would be entrepreneurs: "Get a lot of advice, but don't feel like you're a slave to every piece of advice you get. I networked like crazy. I had never raised venture capital, so I talked to lot of people who had done that. Some of the advice I got was on target. Some of it wasn't."

By 2004, the company changed their name to Constant Contact and in October 2007 completed its initial public offering. Today, the company has over 150,000 worldwide clients that depend on its Web-based email marketing service to communicate with their customers. Reflecting on her years as CEO Goodman said, "My most rewarding business moment ... was reaching 100,000 customers and having a really fun party." And "my scariest business moment ... happened in summer 2001 with less than one payroll in the bank, writing the shutdown plan. It was just a very dark week or two."

Constant Contact's customers span the range, beginning with an unlikely category - churches. Bethany Church of the Nazarene has an active, dedicated congregation the church inspires through innovative and creative communications. Bill Miller, their communications pastor made it his mission to update the way they communicated their message to the congregation. Since they started sending out their new monthly newsletter, the church has experienced a tremendous increase in the number of people signing up. Not only does their newsletter reach 3,000 opt-in subscribers weekly but it also reaches people in multiple countries. "It is an incredible feeling to know that people in another country want to be a part of our extended family," said Bill. "Knowing that the news of our congregation and the work we're doing has a far greater reach through our newsletter than it ever could have otherwise is encouraging and has a positive effect on everyone involved with Bethany."

CRM for Sales

In most companies the largest single expense is sales. As a result much of the initial focus of traditional CRM companies, like Siebel and the leading application cloud service company, salesforce.com, has been building software to increase sales productivity. CRM for Sales seeks to standardize the sales process and make it repetitive. Whether it's having visibility to a lead by status, the lead conversion%, converted leads by month or who is the tops sales rep this class of software has been adopted by small, medium and large enterprises.

Salesforce.com Story

The largest and most visible player in the application cloud service market has been Salesforce.com. Marc Benioff founded Salesforce.com in 1999 to pursue a simple idea: deliver enterprise applications on the Web. With that vision, and with a team of three software developers, Marc founded Salesforce.com. The company began, not in a garage, but in a rented San Francisco apartment, next door to his home. It received no venture capital investment, but was funded instead

by Marc and Larry Ellison. Marc gave his company a mission—
to bring about the end of traditional software. Everywhere he
went he wore a pin that had the word software crossed out. At a
now-famous keynote speech, Marc constantly changed from a
business suit to a Hawaiian shirt and debated himself on the
merits of the old and new ways to deliver software.

From those early days, Salesforce.com's growth has been
meteoric and has symbolized the movement to software on
demand. "Our growth validates the belief in 'The end of
software,' as well as raises new questions for existing software
companies," says Marc. The company made an Initial Public
Offering in 2004 and, by 2005, was generating over $150M in
revenue. In 2009, they were the highest valued of all of the
application cloud service companies. There will be a few stories
about salesforce.com throughout the book. For the insider's view
of the creation of salesforce.com check out Marc's new book[3].

CRM for Service
Once you have a customer keeping a customer is increasingly
defined by the quality of the service delivered. We all know that
high quality service is relevant information, personal to you,

---

[3] Benioff, M., Behind the Cloud: The Untold Story of How Salesforce.com Went from Idea to Billion-Dollar Company-and Revolutionized an Industry, Jossey-Bass (October 19, 2009).

delivered, as you need it. Whether thru web, chat, email or phone, service is all about information.

At the highest level, the U.S. economy is a service economy. Figure 2.1 shows the dramatic shift from manufacturing and agriculture to services over the last 50 years.

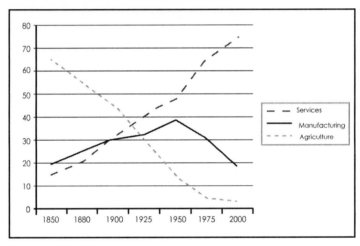

Figure 2.1 Growth of the U.S. Services Economy

Today's services economy accounts for 80 percent of the U.S. GDP (gross domestic product). Financial services, healthcare, education, IT services, and software are all industries that don't manufacture or grow a single thing. Furthermore, contrary to conventional wisdom, this shift has not been an increase in the number of kids flipping hamburgers. Instead, 70 percent of the service employment involves highly skilled people. This includes executives, scientists, and administration and management functions. Figure 2.2 shows the results of the 1996 census.

High-skill Autonomous	40%	Executive, Scientist
Semi-Autonomous	30%	Admin, Manager
Labor Intensive	25%	Maid, Child Care
Tightly Constrained	5%	Call Center, Fast Food

Figure 2.2 United States Census (1996)

Services economy jobs include software designers, hedge fund managers, doctors, lawyers, and customer service professionals and all of these jobs are fundamentally different than working on the assembly line in the early 20th century.

One of the earliest companies to focus on customer service application was RightNow Technologies.

RightNow Technologies Story
Founded by Greg Gianforte in 1997, RightNow went public in August 2004. Based in Bozeman, Montana, RightNow focused on helping customer service organizations improve service delivery using technology. Gianforte didn't start RightNow with venture capital, and makes a passionate case for

starting businesses the old fashioned way. He published a book[4] in which he builds a strong case against relying on venture capital (VC) funding:

- *Raising money takes time away from understanding your market and potential customers. Often more time than it would take to just go sell something to a customer. Let your customers fund your business through product orders.*

- *Money removes spending discipline. If you have the money you will spend it—whether you have figured out your business model and market or not.*

- *You sell your precious equity very dearly before you have a proven business model. This is the worst time to raise money from a valuation perspective.*

Gianforte knows he is pushing a contrarian view, but he reminds the reader that Dell, HP, and Microsoft all originally started without VC funding. In RightNow's case, they doubled their revenues and employees every 90 days for two years before they took any outside money, and, even then, the employees retained more than 75 percent ownership after the company raised $32M.

RightNow provides a suite of customer service and support solutions that captures, tracks, assigns, and manages customer

---

[4] Gianforte, G. "Bootstrapping Your Business: Start and Grow a Successful Company with Almost No Money." BookSurge Publishing, 2007

service interactions from initial contact through resolution. Using their case management, Web self-service, email management, and collaboration modules, companies can more effectively deliver support and service for their customers. Some of RightNow's customers include Ken Harris, CIO at Shaklee, a 50 year old natural nutrition company; Boyd Beasly, Senior Director of Customer Support at EA, a $3B+ leader in electronic gaming and Chuck Udzinski, Consumer Services Manager at Black & Decker, a $6B+ manufacturer of power tools.

"Delivering applications as a cloud service is more than just another way to implement software. It fundamentally changes both the relationship between the software vendor and the customer, and the economics of purchasing and owning software," says Gianforte. "Customers want solutions that are up and running in days or weeks, not months or years, and they are looking for ways to reduce overall ownership costs. Utilizing cloud delivery models, organizations are able to get these advantages over on-premise applications. The cloud is altering the way enterprise applications are being consumed, and today we are just in the early stages of this next evolutionary stage for software."

Vertical Applications

Reading Jared Diamond's bestseller, "Guns, Germs and Steel: The Fates of Human Societies,"[5] may make you see the world a little differently. Diamond's book centers around answering a question he was asked by his New Guinea friend Yali: "Why is it that you white people developed so much cargo [goods] and brought it to New Guinea, but we black people had little cargo of our own?" The answer is that, due to conditions in a few isolated places in the ancient world, some peoples began to produce food either through herding large mammals or growing crops. The lucky ones had the right circumstances to do both. Being a food producer meant that the population could grow. Having the ability to store food meant that the society could develop specialization.

Specialization meant technology could develop. Some people could make weapons, others could grow food, and still others could erect buildings. This is no surprise to us in the modern world of work, but what does specialization mean in software, and why does specialization matter? Probably the best example of the power of specialization is Google. No one had to teach anyone how to use the system; it became immediately obvious what it did and, to the teams building the software, what they

---

5 Diamond, Jared, "Guns, Germs, and Steel: The Fates of Human Societies", W.W. Norton & Co.; 1 edition (July 11, 2005)

needed to do. If Google had started out to build software that enabled you to buy a book, auction a Pez dispenser and search, we're sure history would be quite different. So how specialized can software get? We're conditioned to think that business software is about ERP and CRM, that if we provide purchasing, HR, financial, and sales force automation solutions, we've built all the software a business needs. But if you walk into any ongoing business, you'll discover that the ERP/CRM footprint is less than ten percent of their overall software. Consider the fact that CitiGroup today employs more programmers than SAP or Oracle.

A slightly tongue in cheek example of specialized software is Flock IT.

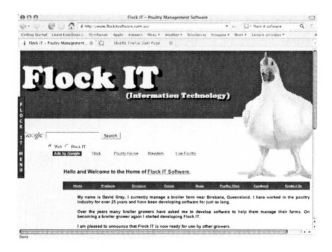

Figure 2.3 Specializations

Flock IT is a company specialized in poultry management software. In the not so distant past, the cost of supporting and selling this software (pre-Internet) would have been so high that the founder could only support customers in his hometown of Brisbane, Australia. Had he wanted to expand to Sydney, he would have had to hire a support engineer and a salesperson. Unless he had enough capital and a high enough price on the software, he just couldn't afford to do this. Search Yahoo! or Google and you'll find thousands and thousands on Flock IT-like companies.

But post-Internet, do we have to think this way? On a global basis, are there not enough people managing poultry to use this software? And once you see this possibility, doesn't the future look like lots and lots of specialized software: search, auctioning, cattle management, pig management, and poultry management software?

There are many examples of specialized applications including those provided by Blackbaud for nonprofit organizations, Dealertrack for automotive dealerships and Opentable for reservation taking restaurants.

DealerTrack Story

DealerTrack was founded in January 2001 with the initial
financing of $20M coming from three forward thinking financial
institutions: J.P. Morgan Chase & Co., AmeriCredit Corp., and
Wells Fargo & Company. They saw whenever a consumer
applied for an auto loan; the old system was both slow and
manually driven, with each lending institution using a different
form—cumbersome for both the consumer and the dealer. In
their first year, DealerTrack brought on line over 20 percent of
the 22,000 dealers in the United States, but by late 2002, a dark
cloud came onto the horizon. Chrysler, Ford and General
Motors decided to finance a new company, RouteOne, to the
tune of $100M. If anything created focus at DealerTrack, it was
this much-needed competition. The company began to add more
dealers (60 percent signed up in year three) as well as more
products for the dealers. DealerTrack went public in 2005, and
today the company is connected to almost all of the 22,000
dealers in the U.S. More interesting, DealerTrack has
established an electronic channel, a real "information
superhighway," that allows them to continue to distribute new
software products, which they are doing at the rate of three per
year.

When Mark O'Neil, Chairman and CEO of DealerTrack, talks about delivering software as a service, he will say there is no other way to run a software business. Not only does he get tremendous economic/cost leverage, which gives him tremendous pricing leverage; but the application cloud service model also gives the company the ability to release new products quickly and nimbly.

Blackbaud Story

Founded by a soccer-playing Englishman, Blackbaud is the market leader in software for non-profit organizations. Their story contains elements of all of the seven business models. First, they have a large support and maintenance revenue stream as a by-product of selling in traditional Model One. In addition a few years ago they began offering their traditional products in Model Four. Below is a chart of the growth of that business.

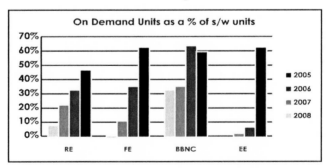

Figure 2.4 Blackbaud's Four Product Lines

Finally, thru acquisitions in 2006 of eTapestry and 2008 of Kintera, Blackbaud has two Model Six companies engineered for multi-tenant low cost delivery.

OpenTable Story

As one of the newest public companies, Opentable is a great example of the blurring of the boundaries between consumer and enterprise software. On the consumer side, OpenTable allows you to find and make reservations at restaurants based on time, date, cuisine, and price range. Upon completing the reservation you receive OpenTable rewards points, which can be redeemed for discounts at member restaurants. On the enterprise side Opentable provides restaurant owners with a reservation management system designed to replace existing paper reservation systems. The solution is an integrated software and hardware solution that computerizes restaurant host-stand operations. The system keeps track of VIPs, customer preferences, integrates with the POS system and allows for re-configuring the tables for larger and smaller seating arrangements. Given the relative unreliability of the network connections this is all implemented on a standalone PC.

In many ways the business looks like a combination of a Model One and a Model Seven business. Sales are done using the traditional door-to-door approach and once the buyer says yes, a consulting arrangement occurs to implement the reservation system. On the other hand the consumer side of the business is a classic Model Seven business. As a diner, you don't pay for the service. Instead Opentable charges the restaurant a monthly fee to be part of the Opentable network as well as a transaction fee that varies depending on whether the reservation originated from Opentable's site or the restaurant's site.

Cloud Service Stack

Many of these application software companies were architected in the late 1990s. But if you were going to start today there is a much larger array of services that you might consider using. We've developed a five-layer stack of services beginning with platform cloud services and including compute & storage cloud services, datacenter services and the original network cloud services.

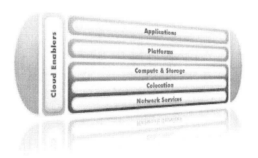

Figure 2.5 Cloud Service Stack

Platform cloud services are either service used by software developers to build new applications (e.g., Microsoft Azure, Google AppEngine or Netsuite's SuiteCloud), or operations staff to manage these application cloud services (e.g., Postini for spam filtering or Service.now for trouble ticketing). Amazon Web Services pioneered compute & storage cloud services, which give you access to computer and storage resources. Compute & storage services use datacenter services to house, power and secure the physical hardware. Finally all of these services are connected thru network cloud services. This organization will serve to frame the next several chapters.

Summary

The early pioneers of SaaS/Application cloud services have demonstrated there is the ability to sell and deliver applications in the new business models. These early pioneers had to build much of the infrastructure and software to deliver and sell these applications. What's exciting today is the creation of 1000s of new cloud services which new providers of applications can now take advantage of. So whether you're taking an existing application and delivering it as a cloud service, developing one for in-house use, or trying to be the next public company the good news is these new cloud services can speed the delivery and lower the cost of getting new applications into the market. The next several chapters will focus on the different layers of this new cloud stack.

3

LOCATION, LOCATION, LOCATION

The compute, storage and network hardware that power all cloud services ultimately must reside in a facility, connected to the network. If you choose to build your own compute and storage cloud service; or if you consume application or platform cloud services this chapter is written to highlight the major areas you'll need to understand.

We'll begin where the name "cloud" began, which are the basic network connection services. We'll move on to discussing one of the key attributes in the reliability and cost of any cloud service: power. Staying with the physical infrastructure, we'll highlight some of the key attributes in building highly available and secure facilities and conclude with the fundamental economics of building data centers. At $1,000 per square foot it's some of the most expensive commercial real estate you'll ever see.

Network Cloud Services

Many have forgotten, but the reason we all call this cloud computing is because we always drew the network (and the Internet) as a cloud. By that we meant, we weren't sure how it worked but somehow bits were transmitted from one point to another, reliably and efficiently.

Clearly, entire books can be written on network cloud service so for our purposes we're going to focus on one valuable idea. Anyone operating an application cloud service will one day need to operate globally, and will require at least one disaster recovery site. If networks were indeed uniformly cheap, reliable and fast then operating out of 2 centers on the planet could work. However, this is not the case so it will be important that the application deployments are location independent. It is here that the world of appliances and application cloud services intersect.

At some point in the day or night, the people managing the application will be remote from the physical location of the computer. If you want the people managing the software to be working the first shift, versus keeping a team in the US on three shifts, then you'll locate people in the Americas, Europe and Asia time zones. Once you've done that, you will need to establish a "Back of the Box" Network to connect the computers to the operations staff, as shown in Figure 3.1.

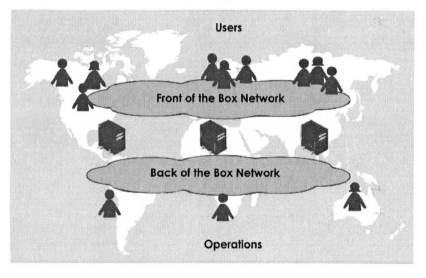

Figure 3.1 Front of the Box, Back of the Box

Your next question will be where to locate the computers. If you want to provide for a disaster recovery site, you'll need at least two sites. Beyond that, you'll need to figure out where your users are concentrated, and the cost, performance and reliability

59

of your "Front of the Box" Network. Companies like Akamai have built a large business helping companies provide more reliable, faster connections. But, in the end, if you're application needs to run in Chile, the cost of bandwidth might be such that you'll need to locate the computers in Chile. Again, this should be no problem if you have architected a location-independent application.

Furthermore, as soon as you realize that standardizing the infrastructure of software and hardware to run in Shanghai, San Francisco and Paris is critical to global deployment; it really doesn't matter where the building that houses the computers is located. Furthermore, it becomes only a financing question as to who owns the actual data center. As a result, there is a fine line between application appliances, and a multi-location deployment of any application cloud service. It becomes more a matter of who pays for what, as opposed to the operational technology. There are, of course, some downsides to not being able to keep all of the hardware in a few locations. In particular, it will be more expensive, as it will be much more difficult to take advantage of spare capacity afforded by other users consuming the same compute and storage resources.

NTT Story

While adoption of business applications delivered out of the cloud has lagged in Europe, NTT Europe Online is trying to change all of that. NTT Europe Online is a wholly owned subsidiary of Nippon Telephone and Telegraph, the largest telecommunications company in the world. They provide private cloud services from five data centers across Europe: UK, France, Germany, Spain, and Switzerland. Today their customers' ranges from Web sites such as Nissan Europe to specialized software companies like Aspiren, and EnergySys.

Aspiren, which focuses on business performance management software for local and central governments, contracted with the UK government to provide the National Performance Management Framework (NPMF). As part of the contract they are delivering a service for 408 local government authorities to benchmark and improve performance, share leading practices, deliver efficiency savings, improve service levels, and report electronically to the central government. You can only imagine the cost and complexity of rolling out software to hundreds local government offices in the traditional Model One world—or should we say—the help desk phone would probably have melted.

EnergySys provides carbon-reporting and accounting software for the oil and gas industry. One of their customers is the South Caucasus Pipeline Company Limited, which transports gas to markets in Azerbaijan, Georgia, and Turkey. Using the EnergySys solution they were able to go live in months. EnergySys gives their customers the choice of having the application delivered as a cloud service or as an appliance the customers can host themselves. But even if the customer chooses the appliance to be installed "@Customer" EnergSys manages the software and insures changes, performance and compatibility are managed. They also price the appliance the same as the online system—the only difference is a minimum that reflects the cost of a dedicated solution. Peter Black, CEO of EnergySys, who started out the business delivering software in Model One, now says—"I don't know why all software is not delivered as a service". And with NTT Europe Online's help perhaps much more software developed and deployed in Europe will follow Peter's lead.

Power Quality

Computers and networks cannot operate without power, and no matter how reliable your electric grid, there is always the possibility you will lose power. During the past decade, there have been several efforts to assess the national cost of power interruptions and power quality. The Electric Power Research Institute (EPRI) estimates the cost at over $119B per year.[6] EPRI, and the National Power Lab data also shows that a typical facility will on average have a voltage fluctuation lasting between one cycle to over thirty minutes 38 times per year. In fact at least 4 times per year the power will be out for a minute or more.

As a result, quality data centers will be equipped with UPS and diesel generators. You should, of course periodically run a test to see if the generators are working—and make sure you run the test long enough. A few years ago, a large data center had to rely on their diesel generators. After two minutes, the systems failed, even though they had tested the generators every quarter. It turned out their quarterly test duration was for 30 seconds. Unfortunately there was a clog in the fuel line, but during testing there was enough fuel in the line to run the test for 30 seconds, and no more.

Power Utilization Efficiency

While having high quality power is important, as we will see the effective usage of power has both economic and carbon

---

[6]The Cost of Power Disturbances to Industrial and Digital Economy Companies. Madison WI. (TR-1006274, Available through EPRI). June 29, 2001,

impacts. The Power Usage Effectiveness[7] (PUE) metric is defined as the ratio of the total power consumed by a data center to the power consumed by the IT equipment that populates the facility. PUE was established by The Green Grid, an association of IT professionals seeking to dramatically raise the energy efficiency of data centers through a series of short-term and long-term proposals. To give you a sense of the range of possibilities, the Uptime Institute gathered data from many of the 85 members of the Institute's Site Uptime Network®. In their sample size the average PUE was 2.58.

In another published work[9] a team from the Lawrence Berkeley National Labs benchmarked 22 data centers. Their analysis showed data centers could be over 40 times as energy intensive as conventional office buildings. They created a metric defined as the Computer Power Consumption Index, which as it turns out is the inverse of the PUE. Figure 3.2 shows the Computer Power Consumption Index for all 22 data centers in their study. The 22 data centers ranged from a PUE of 1.5 to 3.0.

---

[7] The Green Grid, 2007, "The Green Grid Data Center Power Efficiency Metrics: PUE and DCiE," Technical Committee White Paper.
[8] Data Center Energy Efficiency and Productivity By Kenneth G. Brill , Presented at The Uptime Institute Symposium 2007
[9] Best Practices for Data Centers: Lessons Learned from Benchmarking 22 Data Centers Steve Greenberg, Evan Mills, and Bill Tschudi, Lawrence Berkeley National Laboratory Peter Rumsey, Rumsey Engineers Bruce Myatt, EYP Mission Critical Facilities

Computer Power: Total Power

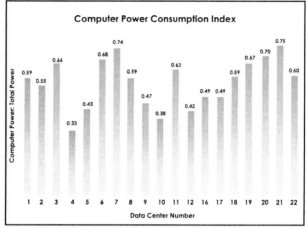

Note: all values are shown as a fraction of the respective data center total power consumption.

Figure 3.2: Computer Power Consumption Index for 22 Data Centers (Inverse of PUE)

Again, because large Model 7 companies consume large numbers of servers per employee it makes sense that companies like Google are pushing the state of the art. Figure 3.3 summarizes the PUE from all Google-designed data centers with an IT load of at least 5MW and time-in-operation of at least 6 months.

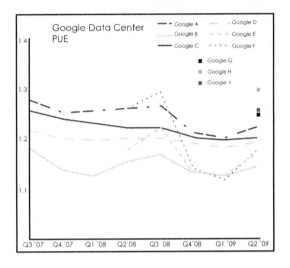

Figure 3.3: Google Data Center PUE

Why is there variation among the data? Power and cooling architectures differ between facilities, and the facilities themselves are located in different climates, which influences the PUE performance. Also, the data centers shown were built at various times since 2005, and over time their designs have become more efficient. For example, Data Center A is the oldest facility of the group and has one of the highest average PUE values. Data Centers E and F are two of the newest and have among the lowest values. In addition, PUE values are impacted by seasonal weather patterns, and thus the PUE during cooler quarters tends to be lower than in warmer ones.

Power Carbon Footprint

With the increasing cost of power and the need to reduce carbon emissions, the other major area of focus is the reduction of overall power and cooling requirements. Dr. Jonathan G. Koomey completed a study on the global power consumption of servers. The total power used by servers represented about 0.6 percent of total U.S. electricity consumption in 2005. When cooling and auxiliary infrastructure are included, that number grows to 1.2 percent, an amount comparable to color televisions' power consumption. In total power demand, this is equivalent to about five 1000-MW power plants for the U.S. and 14 such plants for the entire world. The total electricity bill for operating those servers and associated infrastructure in 2005 was about $2.7B and $7.2B for the U.S. and the world, respectively.[10]

Not all power is created equal. Some power has a much higher carbon footprint than other. For this answer we turn to the Emissions & Generation Resource Integrated Database[11] (eGRID). eGRID is a comprehensive source of data on the environmental characteristics of almost all electric power generated in the United States.

---

[10]Koomey, Jonathan. *Estimating Total Power Consumption by Servers in the U.S. and the World.* Stanford University, February 15, 2007.
[11] http://cfpub.epa.gov/egridweb/

The annual total output emission rate is the measure of the carbon emissions as it relates to the generation output. Units are in lb/MWh and are converted to lb/Watt-year by multiplying by 0.00876. If you go thru the database you will find specific power plants that range from 0 to 876-lbs/watt year. Surprisingly there are coal-fired plants that are cleaner than some oil-fired plans. If you know which specific power plant your data center is connected to then that CPF can be used, otherwise eGRID divides the country into a number of sub-regions.

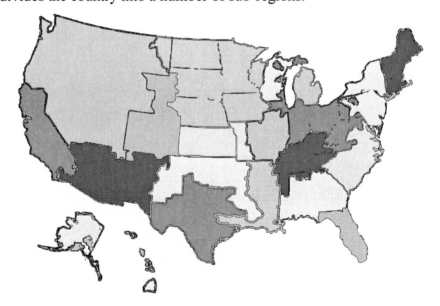

Figure 3.4: Sub-region power grids

Interestingly the sub-regions have a nearly 4:1 difference in the amount of carbon generated per Watt (40-170 pounds/Watt-year).

PG&E Story

Pacific Gas & Electric (PG&E), one of the largest utilities in the United States, is offering significant rebates as part of a new energy incentive program for computer servers. As part of PG&E's Non Residential Retrofit program, customers replacing existing equipment with new servers from Sun Microsystems can receive a cash savings of between $700 and $1000 per server. This is the first-ever incentive rebate offered by a public utility company for servers. Perhaps we'll see more of this in the future.

Availability Management

Whether you decide you need to own your own buildings or just rent, obviously one of the important criteria for a datacenter cloud service is the availability. The Uptime Institute has identified four levels of availability – the best being Tier 4, the lowest level being Tier 1.

Tier 1 data centers have an average outage profile of 1700 outage minutes per year. Tier 1 datacenter cloud services may or may not have UPS, or generators and typically will have only single paths for power and cooling. Tier 2 data centers provide 1300 outage minutes per year and again will typically require maintenance of power to require a shutdown. Tier 3 datacenter services move the outage performance significantly and are designed to deliver 90 outage minutes per year. In order to be able to do this there will be multiple power and cooling distribution paths. Finally, Tier 4 facilities are the top of the heap delivering 26 outage minutes per year.

Security Management

The security of a datacenter cloud service has both a physical and a people component. In general the highly secure facilities will have few windows, a 100-foot vehicle buffer zone, foot thick concrete walls and retractable crash barriers. There will be few entry points and for data centers that are especially sensitive or likely targets, guards may use mirrors to check underneath vehicles for explosives. Surveillance cameras will be installed around the perimeter of the building, at all entrances and exits, and at every access point throughout the building.

This brings us to the people side of the equation. All personnel working in the facility should have background checks. Furthermore using two-factor or biometric identification is becoming standard for access to sensitive areas of data centers. Finally for authenticated individuals, limiting access to areas on a need to access basis.

AT&T Story

In many ways, USi was a creation, and later a victim, of the Internet bubble. Stock in the once publicly held company, reached $66 a share in early 2000. Fleets of jet skis were docked nearby for employees eager for a spin on the Severn River. Payroll ballooned to 1,400 employees. USi raced to build expensive data centers to support the wide range of software it offered.

When the bubble burst, USi was hit hard, ultimately filing for bankruptcy in January 2002. AT&T acquired USi in October 2006 for $300M. Today AT&T's services over 150 clients with end users in over 30 countries. HealthMedia, Inc. is a good example of a software company that used AT&T's datacenter services. HealthMedia's software application provides online programs that focus on disease management (e.g., diabetes), pain management (e.g., arthritis, lower back pain), weight management, and other wellness programs. Companies like Jenny Craig, GlaxoSmithKline, Pfizer, and UPS provide some of these programs to their employees. Since they are in the health care industry, the company must comply with several unique requirements, including the Health Insurance Portability and Accountability Act (HIPAA) and Title 21 Code of Federal

Regulations. As a small company there was no way compliance was possible, but leveraging the scale and expertise of AT&T they could focus on their software and leave the data center certification to their cloud provider.

Economics

Building data centers is expensive. In 2007 Microsoft decided to build a 470,000 sq foot data center at an estimated cost of $550M. In 2008 Amazon.com broke ground on an 116,000 sq foot data center at a cost of $100M. And just so you don't think this is purely a US phenomenon, GDS-China is in the process of building five new data centers in China, with a plan for fifteen more. At ~$1,000 per square foot these are expensive capital investments. In Figure 3.5 you'll see an IBM estimate of the cost breakdown for the various components. Sixty percent of the cost is mechanical and power systems.

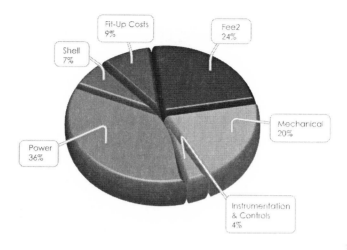

Figure 3.5 Datacenter Capital Costs

This brings us to the on-going operational costs of a data center. Figure 3.6 is an analysis done by IBM which shows what many who have been students of this area already know. That is, that power or energy costs dominate the operational costs of a data center.

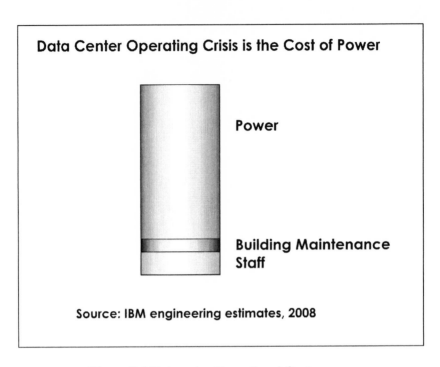

Figure 3.6 Datacenter Operational Costs

Christian Beladay's analysis[12] shows that as of 2008 energy costs alone have exceeded server costs. Moreover the cost of power can fluctuate by a factor of at least 6x, from 3 cents per KWh in Idaho to 18 cents in Hawaii. So in the end it may turn out that future data centers will just be value add to anyone generating power.

---

[12] Belady, C. "In the Data Center, Power and Cooling Costs More than IT equipment it supports", Electronics Cooling Magazine.

Summary

Network and datacenter cloud services represent significant capital investments to build out. Increasingly the location of the data centers will be dictated not only by the proximity to networks, but also by the availability of low-cost, low-carbon high quality power. These data centers will in many ways be the bridges and roads of the next generation of all industries. Utilizing these datacenter cloud services the next layer of the stack is to provide compute and storage cloud services, i.e., providing computers and storage technology purchased by the hour, or the month. We'll discuss this more on the next chapter.

COMPUTE & STORAGE CLOUD SERVICES

The cover story in Business Week in November 2006 was entitled Jeff Bezos' Risky Bet[13]. The article focused on Bezos' vision of transforming the Internet retail giant into a cloud service provider. It started with the Amazon eCommerce API and Alexa Web Search services. But not until the Simple Storage Service (S3) rolled out, did it start to become a reality and with the creation of Elastic Compute Cloud (EC2), Amazon began another revolution.

---

[13] Jeff Bezos' Risky Bet, Business Week November 2006

Compute & Storage Cloud Services

Amazon's Elastic Compute Cloud (EC2) and Simple Storage Service (S3) were the first compute and storage cloud services. Compute cloud services allows scalable deployment of applications by providing a web service through which a user creates a virtual machine instance containing a wide-range of software. Typically these virtual machines include pre-configured Solaris, Windows, or Linux images. While pioneered by Amazon, compute cloud services are now available from Microsoft, Rackspace and GoGrid.

A compute cloud service enables people to create, launch, and terminate server instances as needed, paying by the hour, starting at around $0.10. Some services also provide control over the geographical location of instances, which allows for latency optimization and high levels of redundancy. Also these new compute cloud services will allow you to choose the size of memory as well as the number of virtual cores, all for an increase in the hourly fee.

Along with compute services are storage services. In fact Amazon's S3 pre-dates the availability of EC2. Storage cloud services provide "unlimited online storage" again in a subscription model (typically $0.15/GB/month). Very typically the storage services keep data in at least two, if not three different data centers. The cost of online storage is dramatically lower than tape; hence this architecture precludes the need to provide tape backup and offsite storage.

Amazon Story

At the 2007 Web 2.0 conference, Jeff Bezos delivered the keynote speech and shared some pretty astounding numbers for S3, including a peak day when there were 921 million requests. The number of Amazon Web Service users has grown from 240,000 in 2007 to 540,000 in Q1 of 2009, and in the same time period the number of storage objects has gone from five billion in 2007 to over fifty billion.

In keeping with their growing sophistication in 2008, EC2 provided a service level agreement, a formal commitment that the service will be available at least 99.95 percent of the time. With growing usage also comes growing sophistication in the management infrastructure.

Chief Technology Officer Werner Vogel described some of Amazon's continued investment in reliability and manageability: "We relentlessly measure every possible resource usage parameter, every application counter, and every customer's experience. Many gigabits per second of monitoring data flow continuously through the Amazon networks to make sure that our customers are getting serviced at the levels they can expect and at efficiency level the business desires."

Beyond S3 and EC2 Amazon introduced other services including CloudFront, SimpleDB, and Public Data Sets. CloudFront caches high-traffic content on the company's worldwide network of edge locations so it's always near the end-user for low latency. Customers store the original versions of content (photos, video, music, applications, etc.) into S3, call up an API that returns a unique domain name for the content, then link to it on a Web site or Web application. Amazon has 14 edge locations around the world including Dallas, Los Angeles, Miami, Newark, Palo Alto, Seattle, St. Louis, Amsterdam, Dublin, Frankfurt, London, Hong Kong, and Tokyo. SimpleDB is a new service providing simple relational database service. SimpleDB general manager, Matt Domo says, "Amazon SimpleDB eliminates complexity so that developers and businesses can focus on optimizing applications and not administering their database."

In addition to their own efforts, Amazon is creating a partner community that is further extending their cloud capability. Vertica Systems offers their highly scalable, columnar DBMS on EC2. It enables customers to automatically configure in a matter of minutes analytic databases of virtually unlimited size and performance at a fraction of the cost of conventional systems. Jerry Held, Chairman of Vertica, has been a major figure in the evolution of database technology. As a Ph.D. student at Cal he worked on the relational database that would come to be known as Ingres. He was one of the first developers at Tandem Computers and wrote the original file system and ultimately he went on to preside over Oracle's billion-dollar database business. With that breadth of experience he joined Vertica as Chairman of the Board and has been instrumental in moving them towards the cloud. Jerry says, "The combination of Vertica's ultra high performance at extremely low price and EC2's dynamic configurability are enabling business changing analytics that haven't previously been conceivable. Bringing analytic applications on-line in hours rather than weeks or months and having access to huge resources for varying durations means that what would have been a multi-million dollar capital investment can be turned into a short term, small, opex decision which can be made by line management." And he should know.

But these cloud services are not only being used by new startup companies but also by Fortune 500 corporations including Eli Lilly and Autodesk. "This is a huge step forward in maximizing our results relative to IT spend, and now that Amazon EC2 runs Windows and SQL Server, we have even greater flexibility in the kinds of applications we can build in the AWS cloud," said Dave Powers, an Eli Lilly associate information consultant who uses the service to process research data. "Autodesk uses EC2 for back-end data processing tasks," said Mike Haley, a senior architect of search engineering.

Further signaling the progress they are making was the recent announcement from Capgemini. Capgemini will offer business users Microsoft Sharepoint, Oracle ERP and application development and testing in the cloud. In principle Capgemini is running a Model Three business but using Amazon's compute and storage cloud to offer its outsourcing clients a lower cost approach to pilot projects and IT projects. According to Andrew Gough, SaaS business development manager at Capgemini. "Every business has a project that never surfaces because 80% of an IT budget goes on maintenance," Gough said.

Virtual Machine

Compute cloud services are provided as virtual machine instances. A virtual machine allows the sharing of the underlying physical machine resources between different virtual machines, each running its own operating system. The software layer providing the virtualization is called a virtual machine monitor

CLOUD

or hypervisor. VMWare is the leading company in providing this type of software, although many other companies including Microsoft and Oracle are providing their own. Amazon uses a variation of the Zen open source implementation to deliver their cloud services.

Virtual machines are very useful in situations where the server utilization is low as it allows fewer servers to be shared, thereby reducing power, cooling and space requirements. Figure 4.1 shows the server utilization across a typical data center.

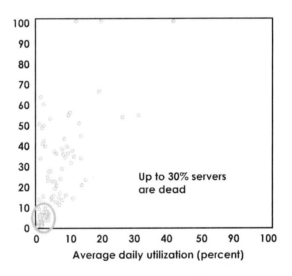

Figure 4.1 Server Utilization in Data Centers

As a result, even in non-cloud implementations virtual machines are being used for server consolidation as a means of reducing cost, and in some cases carbon impact.

Security Management

As more compute & storage service providers enter the market, some will differentiate purely on price, others on quality of service and still others by geographic or industry specializations. One area of particular customer concern is security management. When providing security management at the compute and storage level one needs the ability to robustly authenticate anyone with logical or physical access; provide fine-grained access control and finally audit the interactions. As a result some vendors are providing dedicated VLANs, sub-administrators (so there can be one master account, but multiple groups using it), role-based user permissions and the ability to track actions by department. Furthermore since one of the major principles of good security management is auditability, standards like SAS 70 Type I and Type II, HIPAA (for healthcare) and PCI (for payment) compliance further differentiate one offering from another.

.

TD Banknorth Story

As a financial institution, TD Banknorth's evaluation of vendors' offerings had to be more thorough than most.

Regulations imposed by the Office of the Comptroller of the Currency, for example, set forth strict guidelines about what constitutes appropriate due diligence in such a selection process. In the end, they chose the RightNow service, and particularly important for TD Banknorth was the SAS 70 report. Mark Ellis, Senior Vice President of eCommerce at TD Banknorth, said they "especially liked the fact that RightNow uses AT&T's facilities, which are subject to regular SAS 70 Level II audits."

This, perhaps, makes a more important point. Anyone delivering services in Models Four through Model Seven can make investments in security on behalf of many customers and, as a result, can arguably provide even higher levels of service than any one customer could on their own.

Public and Private Clouds

Being able to control security, specification and performance of the compute and storage infrastructure has given rise to the terminology of public vs. private clouds. Some would say that private clouds are just a marketing term to rename a company's existing data center. While this may be true it's better again to see the range of possibilities as a continuum rather than a black and white decision. Public clouds, like public swimming pools, are specified by the service provider. Of course within those specifications the providers continue to provide increasing degrees of flexibility and security, e.g., greater degrees of control on who has access to what. Early implementations of the public cloud didn't allow you to insure there was capacity when you needed it; however, more recently the idea of reserved instances has been implemented where the user can lock away compute capacity for a year or even three years.

However, if the specification of the cloud service does not fit your needs then, just like with swimming pools, it's clearly possible to implement private clouds. As an example consider JDA Software's market for implementation of its AS/400 E3 product. With nearly 1000 customers worldwide, an implementation of a highly standardized AS/400 compute and storage private cloud would clearly reduce the cost and improve the reliability for any of their customers.

.

IBM Story

In February 2009, IBM's CEO Sam Palmisano appointed Erich Clementi, to head up cloud computing. IBM rarely makes moves like this for strictly marketing purposes and in many ways it signals IBM's view that cloud computing represents the third major wave of business computing – preceded by client-server and mainframe computing.

But why? In 2009 Erich Clementi presented IBM's analysis of the cloud opportunity. In short, their models predict the market is growing at 28% (2008-2012 CAGR), compared to the traditional IT market, which is growing very slowly (1% for traditional SW and SVCS) or decreasing (-3% for traditional HW). In 2012, they predict the cloud opportunity is substantial ($126B), and composed by three sub-markets:

1. Components: $44B. Includes all hardware, software and services purchased by enterprises and direct cloud providers to provide application, platform, compute & storage cloud services to internal or external customers. In effect this is being in the arms dealer business selling traditional hardware and software.
2. Infrastructure services: $30B. Includes the revenue derived by providers of platform, compute & storage cloud services. Within compute & storage cloud services a large portion of business will be driven by clients not buying new physical infrastructure, especially commodity x86 servers and storage, but using public or private services. Here the shift from traditional to new will appear to be even more dramatic, as buying behavior shifts from one time investments to small portions of recurring (or even non-recurring) revenue, e.g. multiples of 10 cents per hour acquired by many individuals unpredictable over the year.
3. Business services: $52B. Includes all applications and any business process outsourcing built on top of application cloud services. As an example IBM uses Taleo to provide certain HR BPO services.

In the long-term, solutions for various industry verticals and small to medium businesses (SMBs) will benefit dramatically from the new economics. IBM is developing and delivering cloud services across the spectrum. These services include a compute & storage cloud service for their Global R&D labs, a new horizontal platform service called Pangoo (developed in IBM's China Research Lab) and application cloud services like LotusLive. Lotus Live is a collaboration tool that lets people share contacts and documents, hold online meetings, and build social-networking communities. Other application cloud services include Rational AppScan OnDemand, for software testing, and Telelogic Focal Point, an online software management tool. At IBM's size and reach and with their treasure trove of technology anyone interested in cloud computing will need to know what they're up to.

New Cloud Applications

Some might see the choice between these new compute and storage cloud services and the traditional model of buying servers and putting them in the data center as purely economic, but to see compute and storage only in this light would be to miss the true potential. Let us suggest three styles of applications that can truly benefit from the new model: very high growth applications; peaky applications and parallel applications.

The first category of applications is very high growth applications. Only one out of a thousand applications might see rapid adoption, but when you hit the lottery, the ability to rapidly scale is critical. Consider Animoto, an online service that allows you to create video productions simply. You upload your photos or Powerpoint, choose a song and Animoto creates an effects-heavy movie in minutes. When it launched on Facebook, demand was such that it had to increase the number of compute instances on Amazon's EC2 from 50 to 3500 within three days. "You could give me unlimited funding," says Adam Selipsky, VP at Amazon Web Services, "and I wouldn't know how to deploy that many servers in 72 hours"[14]

Peaky Applications

Peaky applications are characterized by cyclic resource usage; computations that occurs every day, but not every night; or every week or every month. In this scenario, the traditional model requires allocating the largest required resource, even though it might only be used 1/3 of the period.

Consider a Wall Street firm where they upload the day's market trading data into a storage service every evening, and run

---

[14] Economist - October 25, 2008- A Special Report on Corporate IT

proprietary risk management algorithms. The analysis typically lasts ~10 hours and 3000 compute instances are used. That is an order magnitude greater than the daytime and weekend workload of 300 instances.

Parallel Applications

As part of teaching the first class on cloud computing at Tsinghua University, Amazon donated $3000 worth of time on the Amazon cloud. At $0.10 per hour, you could use one instance continuously for 3.5 years, 100 computers for 12 days or 10,000 computers for 30 minutes. But what would you do with 10,000 computers for 30 minutes? We've never been able to ask that before. The answer promises to be truly exciting.

Only two areas in business computing have taken advantage of large numbers of independent, low cost computers. In the 80s, Tandem Computers created systems that allowed 256 computers to outperform the most powerful mainframes of the era in a transaction processing system, which was optimized to enable parallel execution. Beginning in 2000, Google used the power of thousands of computers to enable low cost, high performance search. The challenge is to identify (and parallelize) algorithms that are not as simple as consumer search.

CLOUD

One of the chief architects of the Tandem system, Jim Gray,
in more recent years turned his attention to what he called the
"fourth paradigm" of science[15]. The first three paradigms were
experimental, theoretical and computational science. The Fourth
Paradigm is driven by our ability to capture a huge amount of
data – whether the human genome or an interlocking web of 300
million people's social graphs. Jim's vision is that eScience can
unify theory, experiment, and simulation with a new generation
of applications specifically designed to manage, visualize and
analyze this even deeper Web of data. Based on low cost
compute and storage services Jim saw a world in which all
science literature, all science data could interoperate online.
Sadly, in 2007 Jim disappeared in his boat off of the coast of
California. While his future contributions will be missed – he
has certainly put yet another stake in the ground for what might
be.

HP Story

HP has formed a joint cloud computing effort called the
Cloud Computing Test Bed (CCTB) that will allow researchers
from allied academic institutions and industry to test software
written for cloud infrastructure. It will provide a large cloud-
computing infrastructure where people can test distributed

---

[15] "The Fourth Paradigm: Data-Intensive Scientific Discovery." Edited by Tony Hey, Stewart
Tansley and Kristin Tolle. Microsoft Research.

software at all levels of the stack, from low-level OS, storage, and networking technologies all the way up to user-facing applications. The CCTB will consist of six sites, each of which will house about 1,000 to 4,000 processor cores. When those six initial centers are ganged together, the resulting cloud will have a core count that should put it somewhere in the Top 20 supercomputers list. This compute and storage cloud uses HP hardware and software and runs Yahoo's Apache Hadoop, an open source platform that lets users write and run applications that process vast amounts of data.

Today's Clouds are Small

Google's cloud contains over 500,000 servers. Many see that as large – but is it really? The NYSE stock trading system processes about 10M trading transactions per day. Visa is believed to process around 100M credit card authorization transactions and Google about 200M searches per day. But, consider if every mobile phone in the world executed just one transaction per day you'd have to process over 4,000M transactions per day.

IBM projects that by 2011, the world will be ten times more instrumented then it was in 2006 and the number of Internet connected devices will grow from 500M to 1 Trillion. If as Vic Gundotra of Google says the iPhone and Android are merely the "eyes and ears" of the cloud, then the potential number of transactions will only grow. Application such as real time translation, turn-by-turn navigation or determining the supply chain that brought the lettuce in your local market will demand truly large clouds.

21st Century Smokestack: Computer Carbon Footprint

As compute & storage infrastructure grows, the carbon footprint of modern technology-powered companies of the company's computers is 21st Century's smokestack. This section discusses a simple way to calculate a company's Computer Carbon Footprint™ (CCF).

The CCF is computed as follows:

$$CCF = \#Employees \times SPE \times TBY \times PUE_{avg} \times CPF_{avg}$$

Where

SPE = Servers Per Employee

TBY = Technology Birth Year factor X 400 watts

PUE_{avg} = Average Power Utilization Efficiency of the data centers

CPF_{avg} = Average Carbon Power Footprint of the sub-region grids (lbs/watt-year)

Servers Per Employee (SPE)

The number of Servers per Employee may be a simple measure of how much a company is powered by technology.

Interestingly, Simon Commander of the London Business School and Rupert Harrison of the IFS School of Finance measured the number servers per employee in Brazil at 0.04 and in India at 0.02[16]. A 2007 World Bank book[17] on the economy of Columbia reported a range from 0.32 to 3.33 computers per employee.

Of course, nothing compares to modern large-scale Internet companies. In 2006, Google deployed an estimated 450,000 servers.[18] With approximately 10,000 employees in 2006, Google's SPE (Servers per Employee) would be 45.

	Year	Servers Per Employee
India	2007	0.02
Brazil	2007	0.04
Columbia	2007	0.32-3.33
Google	2006	45

Figure 4.2: Servers Per Employee

Technology Birth Year (TBY)

TBY is designed to compute the approximate power consumption of all of the servers. This is done by establishing a base line of power consumption at 2006 at 400 watts and then if

[16] ICT adoption in developing countries: Firm-level evidence from Brazil and India; Simon Commander (London Business School) Rupert Harrison (IFS School of Finance 1st June 2006.
[17] Environmental Priorities and Poverty Reduction: A Country Environmental Analysis for Colombia (Directions in Development) (Paperback) by Kulsum Ahmed (Author), Kulsum Ahmed; Ernesto Sanchez-triana; Yewande Awe (Editor)
[18] Markoff, John and Hansell, Saul. Hiding in Plain Sight: Google Seeks an Expansion of Power. The New York Times, June 14, 2006.

the servers are on average older or younger, increasing or decreasing the power consumption. We base our analysis on a recent paper[19] authored by Jonathan G. Koomey, of Lawrence Berkeley National Labs, Stephen Berard from Microsoft, Marla Sanchez with Stanford University and, Henry Wong from Intel Corporation. The paper explores the relationship between the performance of computers and the electricity needed to deliver that performance. As shown in the figure below, computations per kWh grew about as fast as performance for desktop computers starting in 1981, doubling every 1.5 years, a pace of change in computational efficiency comparable to that from 1946 to the present.

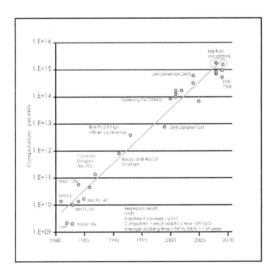

Figure 4.3: Computation per kWH per decade

---

[19] Assessing Trends in the Electrical Efficiency of Computation over Time, Submitted to IEEE Annals of the History of Computing: August 5, 2009 Released on the web: August 17, 2009

Under the above assumption that computations per server doubling every 1.5 years then the same unit of performance would require 4x more power 3 years earlier in 2003 and ¼ the amount of power 3 years later, in 2009.

Technology Birth Year	
2003	4
2004	3
2005	2
2006	1 (Baseline)
2007	0.75
2008	0.5
2009	0.25

Figure 4.4: Technology Birth Year factor

While every server consumes a different amount of power we will use 400 watts as the average power consumption of a server in 2006. This will also make our estimates conservative. More precise calculations would include the data in Figure 4.5.

	2000	2003	2005
Volume	183	214	$218
Mid-range	423	522	$638
High-end	4874	5815	$12,682

Figure 4.5: Weighted average power (Watts) of top 6 servers, by sales[20]

---

[20] Koomey, J., G., 2007, Estimating Total Power Consumption by Servers in the US and the World. February 2007. http://enterprise.amd.com/Downloads/svrpwrusecompletefinal.pdf

Summary

Post the crash of 2001, many companies focused on reducing the cost and as a result gave rise to the first generation of application cloud service companies (Salesforce, Taleo, RighNow...). While these companies have wide applicability, the introduction of compute and storage cloud services has the potential to make an even bigger impact. Again spurred by the economic downturn of 2008 and the tightening of credit anyone looking at deploying new hardware resources (or even upgrading existing infrastructure) has to at least consider this new model of computing. And just as the advent of low cost PCs spurred the last generation of client-server applications, this new generation of compute and storage cloud services promises again to bring a new class of applications we've never seen before. Which brings us to the subject of the next chapter – platform services for new application development.

5

SILVER BULLET

Just as the battle for the desktop was won by winning the developer, so it may be in the fight to win the cloud. This chapter is <u>not</u> written for the VP of R&D at a software company. Instead is meant to give those, who are not experts, a working knowledge of the issues, tools, and economics of software development. We'll cover the fundamentals of the software development lifecycle and touch upon the new horizontal and vertical platform cloud services that provide software developers with tools for the world of cloud computing. We'll see how new technologies are bridging the worlds of new application development, and management, which heretofore have been separate disciplines.

Application Spectrum

Before discussing key success factors, we should note that all applications are not created equal. While all software can be delivered as a service from the cloud, *how* it is delivered will vary according to the software and its usage.

One variation is the application weight.

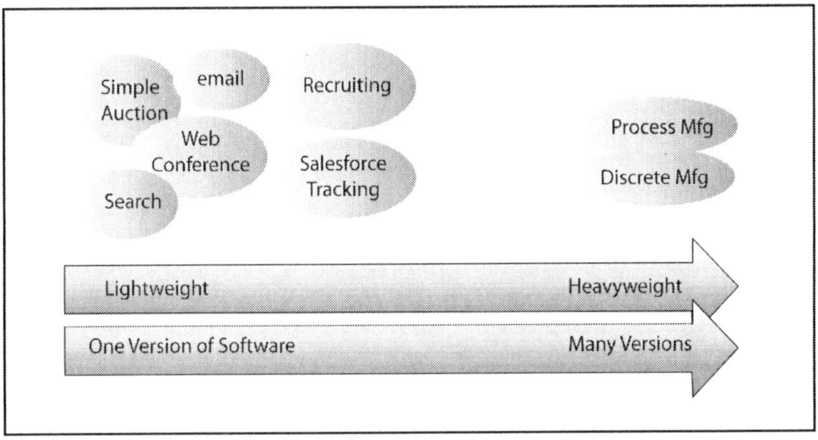

Figure 5.1 Application Weight

By weight we mean the complexity of the business process. Email is a very lightweight business process; each of us uses it similarly. eBay-style auctioning, Web conferencing, Internet search are also lightweight. Discrete and process manufacturing, areas that Oracle and SAP have specialized in, are heavyweight business processes. The way Coca-Cola manufactures soda has little in common with Chevron's petroleum refining process, although both are manufacturing processes. These processes are much more customized. No one knows how to make these as customizable as changing a Yahoo home page. As a result, lightweight business processes have moved to Model Six and Model Seven sooner.

The implications of application weight are many. First, the lightweight business processes allow for greater frequency of change. At one end of the spectrum, manufacturing or financial applications deployed in the traditional model have resulted in upgrades occurring every couple of years, often at great expense. At the other end is eBay making changes 52 times a year.

Another evaluation you'll need to make designing the applicationis to map the number of users for your software against the frequency of use. This usage spectrum is shown in Figure 5.2.

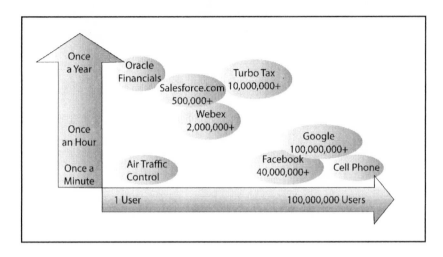

Figure 5.2 Usage Spectrum

Corporate applications, like SAP Financial Applications, usually have very few users, all of whom use the application infrequently. The closer you get to the consumer Internet, the greater the number of users and frequency of use and consequently, the degree of specialization and focus for the application. Where the application fits in this continuum has many implications for software development and delivery.

Multi-tenancy

One area that is hotly debated is that of a single-tenancy versus multi-tenancy model. If you're coming from the world of traditional enterprise software, you only architected for single-tenancy. Adopting Model Four or Five allows software, architected for Model One, to be deployed as a service in the cloud. This gives the customer some, but not all, of the flexibility in on-premise deployment. The approach does not require rewriting or building new software and allows one to offer the service to the 100s or 1000s of businesses who have already bought the application.

If you have a lightweight business process and intend to write the application from scratch, you should consider a multi-tenancy model. In this approach, a given table includes records from multiple tenants stored in any order and a tenant ID column associates every record with the appropriate tenant. The multi-tenancy approach allows you to serve the largest number of tenants per database server. However, because multiple tenants share the same database tables, this approach may require additional development effort in the area of security to ensure that one tenant can not access another's data.

More importantly, the multi-tenancy approach requires one code line which vastly simplifies the development and management of the software. eBay, as an example, has maintained one code line since they were founded. Of course, this is possible only in areas with lightweight business processes, and it has exponential advantages when you serve millions of users in a highly fluid environment.

The distinction between multi and single tenancy can be illusionary. Most of the multi-tenancy service providers run multiple sites. Furthermore each of these applications can be on a different revision level. This is often done to do A-B testing of new releases, as well as a change management technique. In the limit, if General Motors wanted one of those sites to run only GM auctions, how is that different than single tenancy?

Bottom line; don't get embroiled in the religious war. There are numerous tradeoffs to be made, depending on whether you're starting with an existing application or building from scratch; whether you have a lightweight or heavyweight business process; and finally the margins and pricing you'll need to be successful in the market.

Underlying this whole debate is a much more fundamental principal that's illustrated in Figure 5.3: dramatically reducing the cost and improving the quality of anything starts with standardization. If something is standardized, you can specialize. Specialization leads to repetition and, ultimately, computers are far better at repetition than people. If you want the highest quality, lowest cost automobile, choose a Toyota, not a McLaren F1. Although, a hand-built automobile with a production run of fewer than 100 cars is exclusive, a $1,000,000 car that needs a McLaren mechanic is neither low cost or high quality. So how does this apply to software?

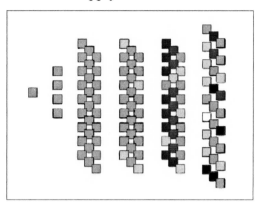

Figure 5.3 Standardization

Every SAP or Oracle enterprise application deployment is different as each installation is on a different server and disk architecture. Each application is also deployed on a different software stack—different versions of operating systems, databases, and middleware. Beyond that, each deployment has different change management or disaster recovery processes implemented by different people. So if we took a paint brush to the current installed base of enterprise applications, every box would be colored a different color, just as every box in Figure 5.3 is slightly different. On the left-hand side of the figure, think about eBay, with three sites, each running the same software, hardware and management processes. All of the states in between represent progressively greater degrees of standardization. Every choice you make in hardware architecture, software architecture, and management processes should be an effort to move closer and closer to the left-hand side. With a greater degree of standardization comes the ability to specialize, repeat, and ultimately automate the greatest cost you have—the human labor required to manage these systems.

Software Development Lifecycle

Few books on software engineering have been as influential as Fred Brooks' *Mythical Man Month*, originally published in June 1975. Much of it was based on his experiences as the development manager of IBM's OS/360-at the time, the largest software development project ever undertaken. He recounts that the project could *not* be considered a success. There were design and execution flaws. The project was late, over budget, and underperformed against expectations for the first several releases.

Brooks documented what came to be known as Brooks' Law: "Adding Manpower to a late software project makes it later." Many people in the software business can testify to personal experiences that validate his comment. He estimated that software project use a $1/3^{rd}$ of their scheduled time in requirements, $1/6^{th}$ in coding, a $1/4^{th}$ in unit testing, and a $1/4^{th}$ in system testing before it would be ready for release. Assuming a

24-month release cycle, you'd spend six months in requirements, three months writing code, and the last 12 months testing - no real surprise to the old-timers.

Brooks later published a landmark paper[21] in which he wrote, "Not only are there no silver bullets now in view, the very nature of software makes it unlikely that there will be any. No inventions that will do for software productivity, reliability, and simplicity what electronics, transistors, and large-scale integration did for computer hardware. We cannot expect ever to see twofold gains every two years." Throughout the past 30-plus years, the industry has struggled to find a way to uncover Brooks' elusive order-of-magnitude improvement in software productivity. Rapid prototyping, object-oriented programming, program verification, and Software Engineering's Capability Maturity Model (CMM) all have been thought to be the "silver bullet". Unfortunately, each attempt has come up short.

While building and deploying high quality software is certainly no easy task, delivery of software as a service is fundamentally changing the way software is designed, developed, and tested. Have we found Dr. Brooks' silver bullet?

---

[21]Brooks, Fred. No Silver Bullet: Essence and Accidents of Software Engineering. IEEE Computer, April 1987.

Horizontal Platform Services

Once you know the kind of application you want to build you'll have to decide how to build it – what your coding framework will be. There are three basic choices: horizontal software, horizontal services, and vertical services.

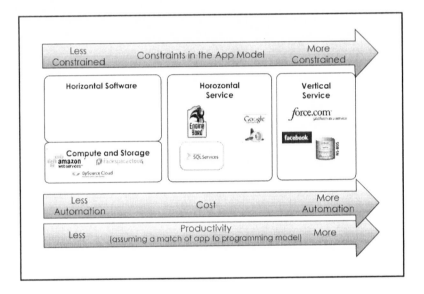

Figure 5.4 Platform Cloud Services

Horizontal software allows any software (open-source or traditional Model 1 software) on a compute and storage cloud service. You can use the database, middleware and languages of your choice. Today's application cloud service providers, who did not have horizontal or vertical platform services to choose from use large amounts of horizontal software on compute and storage services they have to manage.

106

Horizontal platform services offer less flexibility than the roll your own horizontal services. Here the cloud service provider manages the platform software thereby reducing cost and complexity. Restrictions in flexibility (e.g., definition of a particular database schema) result in more vertical platform services that trade flexibility for greater productivity and lower cost assuming you're application maps well to these vertical platform services.

The advantages of these platform services are best understood in the context of traditional application environment. Figure 5.5 shows the traditional silos: the group that writes the original application, the group that ports and tests it in multiple operating system and database environments and the operations management group that manages the application after delivery.

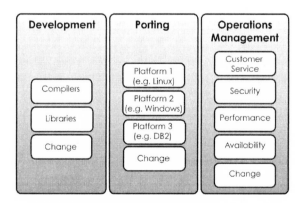

Figure 5.5 Traditional Application Development & Deployment

The new generation of platform services attempts to merge these worlds since now the software builder also operates it. Platform services can:

- Maintain a current level of the underlying software
- Automatically replace a failed server
- Replicate production application for testing and staging with one-button click.
- Automate change management – from code check in to production
- Add capacity when load thresholds trigger.

Heroku is a good example of providing horizontal platform services to the Ruby-on-Rails community. Google's App Engine, while it has a number of programming model restrictions, does give access to the high scalability of Google's compute and storage services. Unlike traditional LAMP stack deployment, App Engine frees you from the operations management hassles like disk space management, security patch management and backup and recovery. Finally, Microsoft, which ruled the client-server programming model, has introduced Azure to provide an easy on ramp for millions of Microsoft programmers around the world to build next generation application cloud services using their familiar tools.

Microsoft Azure Story

In a widely publicized email to top executives, dated Oct. 30, 2005, Bill Gates urged company leaders to "act quickly and decisively" to move further into offering software as services, in order to preempt what he saw as formidable competitors. "This coming 'services wave' will be very disruptive," Gates wrote. "We have competitors who will seize on these approaches and challenge us—still, the opportunity to lead is very clear." Gates compares the push toward such services, which range from online business software offerings to free Web-based email, to the changes he saw nearly a decade ago. Then he wrote a now-famous memo, *The Internet Tidal Wave,* which prompted a massive shift at Microsoft toward Internet-based technology. "The next sea change is upon us," Gates wrote. While Gates might have left day-to-day operational responsibilities, there are key people to carry on his vision. First and foremost is Chief Software Architect, Ray Ozzie. In a recent interview Ozzie said, "We're going to look back at this era and wonder how we did without this other kind of computer in the cloud."

Windows Azure seeks to provide the Microsoft Visual Studio programmer with compute and storage services similar Amazon's together with SQL and .Net services with integrated operations management. For example, the SQL Azure service provides availability monitoring on five minute intervals as well as updating lower level system software as required.

Google AppEngine Story

In mid-2008 Google introduced App Engine. Google Apps provided office applications in the cloud; App Engine attempts to provide a platform for others to build cloud-based applications. At App Engine Campfire One in April 2008, App Engine Tech Lead Kevin Gibbs, said, "App Engine is different than a lot of other things out there. App Engine is not a grid computing solution. We don't run arbitrary compute jobs. We also don't give you a raw virtual machine. Instead, we provide a way for you to package up your code, specify how you want it to run in response to requests, and then we run and serve it for you. You don't reserve resources, or machines, or RAM or a number of CPUs, or anything like that. It's a fluid system that runs your code in response to load and demand."

Ultimately, App Engine's goal is to provide a simpler alternative to the traditional LAMP stack. This more vertical (more constrained) offering hopefully will provide greater productivity despite decreased flexibility. If you want flexibility you can always go buy your own computers.

App Engine requires server side code to be written in Python. You can make use of numerous Python modules and libraries using any Web framework. The database is not SQL. Instead it is based on Bigtable, the system used for Google.com. Bigtable is a fault-tolerant, distributed system that can span tens of thousands of hard disks on thousands of machines, making all of them appear to be a single storage table. It is designed to move data around and restructure the system automatically to account for hotspots and increased storage. Unlike SQL, Bigtable is schema-less, meaning it can support arbitrary new properties or columns, which can be created as you code. One feature you won't find is joins, since they are typically a source of performance problems in a distributed system.

In addition to the programming environment, there is also operations environment. App Engine provides an administration console is provided to give access to the application. Although some early applications are being demonstrated, it is still early days.

Vertical Platform Services

Vertical platform services provide even less programming model flexibility in return for increased productivity and decreased management costs. Vertical platform services assume you are building a specialized use of the wider platform provided by the vertical platform cloud service. This typically means you're leveraging at least the data model and hopefully some of the higher level abstractions provided by that data model.

Good examples of vertical services include Netsuite's SuiteCloud, Salesforce.com's force.com and Facebook's platform. Netsuite allows application builders who want to specialize their ERP oriented platform for more specific markets. Salesforce with force.com provides not only the technology, but a marketplace (AppExchange) to encourage new CRM applications. Finally with so many users of Facebook, by opening up the platform (most notably Facebook Connect) Facebook can extend their services far faster than with their captive R&D group.

Salesforce.com Story

Salesforce.com has led the way in turning their platform into a service others can use. AppExchange was launched in late 2005, ironically almost at the same time that Oracle acquired Siebel. At the time, the objective was to enable customers and partners to customize the Salesforce.com application and extend it. There was no firm plan to extend the core application platform beyond its forms-driven database model. Phil

Wainewright, who blogs about SaaS for ZD Net, writes that two events changed Salesforce.com's approach. The first was an attempt to use the platform to write a quote application, which required transactional integrity. The second was developers beginning to build applications that were not conventional forms-based apps. The result, according to Phil, was the creation of the Apex programming language, ultimately leading to a complete platform for building application cloud services. Apex provides the Force.com platform with a procedural language so that users can go beyond declarative programming to write code where needed.

You can use Apex to create triggers, which fire when any user performs certain data operations. It can also create classes, which can be called from other classes and triggers, enabling productive code reuse and standardization. A year after Apex's introduction, Force.com platform added Visualforce. Visualforce is a framework to build custom user interfaces. The Visualforce framework includes a tag-based markup language, similar to HTML. Underlying the Force.com platform is a multi-tenant database that differs from relational databases in the way record relationships are implemented. Instead of developers' having to deal with keys, foreign keys, primary keys and defining relationships in terms of these keys, the database is organized in terms of relationship fields. A relationship field stores the ID of the parent record in a relationship, as well as optionally providing user interface representations in both the parent and child records. The Force.com platform supports two query languages:

- Salesforce Object Search Language (SOSL) is a language for searching across all persisted objects.
- Salesforce Object Query Language (SOQL) is a query-only language. While similar to SQL in some ways, it's an object query language that uses relationships, not joins, for a more intuitive navigation of data.

Of course, the real test is the types of applications that can be built and delivered using the salesforce.com cloud. Two interesting case studies are Riskonnect and Stakeware. Bob Morrell founded Riskonnect in July 2007. He has a long history in risk management software beginning in 1994 with Risk Laboratory.

Riskonnect's software, launched in 2008, helps people visualize and understand risk at very high levels. "This is essential because too many consultants only use complicated calculations. But many people don't need that," Morrell said. Riskonnect allows users to drag and drop information to compare risks visually. An example would be if one factory goes down, how would other factories and the supply chain respond.

Natan Zaidenweber founded StakeWare in 2004. Zaidenweber has over 15 years of experience as a researcher, lecturer, and manager in sustainability projects for The World Bank, The Mexican Government, and Shell Oil. StakeWare enables corporations to gather, organize, and analyze stakeholder data and identify key issues, related indicators, and relevant material to include in the standard G3 sustainability report. It also includes the ability to monitor and analyze emissions to provide appropriate trade-offs for lowering the carbon footprint and managing the sustainability policies across supply-chain.

Riskconnect and Stakeware are proof that as Marc Benioff said: "Software developers from a developing country can build just as great an application on our platform as somebody who lives in Palo Alto."

Facebook Story

In February 2009, a little more than a month after announcing it had 150 million active Facebookers, Dave Morin, who runs the application platform team, twittered the number was now 175 million. That kind of growth and scale can in part be attributed to Facebook opening up its platform and providing a full suite of APIs—including a network protocol, a database query language, and a text markup language—that allow applications to integrate tightly with the Facebook user experience. Their most recent effort has been to bring the power of Facebook to other applications by providing the ability to:

- Connect any existing Facebook account and information with any application.
- Connect and find friends who also use the application.
- Share information and actions on the application with their Facebook friends.

This is a particularly valuable service since in the cloud many people will not identify themselves. How many times have you signed up for a site or a newsletter with fake identity? On the other hand it's difficult to have a fake Facebook identity. Unless you have no friends, it'll be difficult to pretend you're Angelina or Brad. Not only is basic profile information available but also the profile picture, friends, photos, events, groups, and more.

With access to the social graph, an application can dynamically show which Facebook friends already have accounts on the application. As an individual moves around the Web, their privacy settings will follow them, ensuring that users' information and privacy rules are always up to date. For example, if a person changes their profile picture, or removes a friend connection, this is automatically updated in the application. In addition, the individual can control who can see what pieces of their information—the same rules that they set on Facebook can be applied through your application. If you're interested in seeing early examples of applications using the Facebook platform take a look at TechCrunch, Citysearch, VLane, and Howcast.

Facebook has published a set of principles for their applications. Some of these are clearly unique to their applications—others are just good ideas.

Applications should be meaningful.

- Social – Helps people interact and communicate more effectively by using information from the social graph
- Useful – Delivers value to people by addressing real world needs, from entertainment to practical tasks
- Expressive – Enables people to share more about who they are and about the world around them.
- Engaging – Provides a deep experience that people want to come back to regularly

Applications should be trustworthy.

- Secure – Protects user data and honors privacy choices for everyone across the social graph

- Respectful – Values individual attention and honors their intentions in communications and actions
- Transparent – Explains how features will work and how they won't work, especially in triggering person-to-person communications

Applications should be well designed.

- Clean – Designed to be intuitive, easy to use and free of mistakes
- Fast – Achieves low latency while scaled to handle individual demand
- Robust – Maintains reliable uptime and minimizes error rates

With such a large population of people on Facebook, a successful application on Facebook can grow to millions of people in a short time. A case in point is the story of iLike. When iLike launched 10,000 people joined in the first 12 hours. By the end of the first day it had 50,000 people. In less than a year, iLike announced it had passed three million and were growing at a rate of 300,000 per day. We should all be so lucky.

NetSuite Story

In 2005, NetSuite opened its architecture to partners and outside developers to further its reach through its NetSuite SuiteCloud, a cloud development environment that includes a set of Application Program Interfaces (APIs), a mechanism to distribute applications, and the NetSuite application itself. To use Zach Nelson's words: "By using the cloud, we can now economically reach the Fortune 5,000,000".

As a more vertically focused platform cloud service, SuiteCloud targets building out the core NetSuite offering with additional specialized functionality beyond the services delivered by the core application. The resulting specialized application and data reside inside the NetSuite platform and share database and server resources within the core solution. This tight integration enables the platform and applications to remain in sync as the underlying NetSuite application is upgraded.

The SuiteCloud APIs, give application developers data storage flexibility. Developers can create custom forms to give users access to specific fields, and create completely new custom record types for objects unique to a specialized application. SuiteScript, the JavaScript API, allows developers to add workflow to records and automate business processes for target industries with full transactional integrity. Integration with external systems is supported through SuiteTalk. SuiteTalk uses industry standard SOAP and XML messaging to communicate with external applications. The platform also allows developers to build Web services integrations using .Net, Java or PHP. Finally, the resulting application can be packaged using SuiteBundler, which enables members of the SuiteCloud Developer Network to distribute their applications on SuiteApp.com.

As a result of this strategy NetSuite has focused on specialized developers. "Rather than cast a wide net, we target partners with the industry experience to create compelling applications," says Guido Haarmans, NetSuite VP of Developer Programs. A couple of examples of these specialized applications are those provided by Roostock Software and SPS Commerce. Pat Garrehy, a veteran of the manufacturing and Material Requirements Planning (MRP) software, founded Rootstock. His previous company developed conventional Model One ERP/MRP software that was used by companies like Lockheed and Solectron. In 2008, Garrehy got the itch to return to the MRP business. He recognized the rise of cloud computing and rather than replicate fundamental ERP functionality he chose to build on NetSuite. With NetSuite providing the underlying cloud services, they built a multi-plant MRP application, in just nine months.

SPS Commerce, a leader in electronic data interchange (EDI) supply chain, developed a specialized application that allows smaller suppliers to tap into their network of over 1,300 retailers, thereby allowing a small supplier to quickly and inexpensively meet the complex EDI requirements. Circle of Friends and Mad Croc, both small CPG manufacturers, benefited. Neither could afford traditional ERP and EDI applications and the IT resources necessary to keep them running. But without an EDI solution they were limited in which retailers they could work with. By adopting the vertical application cloud service they could quickly and inexpensively manage their entire trading relationships, from inventory to shipping and invoicing.

Testing

As Fred Brooks noted, most of software development time and cost involves testing. So how does moving to an on-demand model change anything as regards testing and QA? First of all, moving to the model reduces the number of variations and creates greater standardization. Whether that's a standardized delivery model in Model Four or Five, or using one line of code when you move to Models Six or Seven, reducing the degree of freedom reduces the number of overall tests that have to be developed and executed. Now, instead of trying to create and manage tests for this application release (and the three previous releases) and insure that they work on Oracle, IBM and MySQL databases on HP, IBM or Sun hardware, the QA team can limit their focus to one line of code (hopefully), one database, and one hardware platform.

Furthermore, the model lets you begin to leverage tests of specific customer configurations and execute those tests very early in the development cycle. So, rather than wonder whether an upgrade will work, you'll know, since the application will have already been tested in the development labs. Collapsing the supply chain between the customer and the producers of the software has even further economic benefits. Rather than employ an army of test developers in your engineering organization, you can use the actual customer systems to develop real-world tests. The tests are more representative and come at a much lower cost.

But there are also major new responsibilities and issues. For instance, if you introduce a bug into production, 100 percent of your customers experience that bug immediately. Think about that. Concur co-founder Michael Hilton said, "For Concur, that means over six thousand companies and over four million end users are affected by any defect." It has fundamental impacts on how you think about quality assurance. But there's a flip side as well—you can fix the issue and 100 percent of your customers have that issue resolved—no more waiting for the slow trickle of customers to download and install the patch."

Of course, just as we will see in the next chapter on operations, the testing/QA function will need to re-engineer for the new reality of a release a week or a release a month, not a release every 24 months. Again, as Hilton points out, "This fundamentally changes how you develop. You end up releasing things in smaller chunks, so users can easily digest them. And you end up releasing more often. At Concur, we do meaningful functional updates to our service every single month. That means that, every month, our users are getting new innovations and benefits without having to do anything. It forces you to care a lot more about the user experience, ease of use and change management. Lots of things end up being optional, meaning that, if the feature is big enough, customers don't have to deal with it right away if they don't want to."

Customization

One of the major objections to the SaaS/application cloud service model has been the belief that there is no ability to customize. "You can have any color you want as long as it's black," was the famous Henry Ford quote often used by people describing early offerings.

While this subject is almost nonexistent from a consumer perspective, any conversation with corporate IT will inevitably lead to the discussion of how to customize the application. Even though Oracle On Demand was blessed with a natural channel to medium and large-scale businesses, it remained challenged on how to address this question. Some engineers would try to be PC (politically correct) and say, "We don't allow for customization, we allow for configuration." Or others would say, "We don't support extensions, we support configurations." The conversation was confusing. Marian Szefler, today Senior VP of R&D at Risk Management Solutions, architected an innovative approach while at Oracle that changed the argument from techno-babble to a business decision.

In 2000, Marian defined the CEMLI framework. CEMLI stood for Configuration, Extension, Modification, Localization and Integration, and described 17 classes of reason why someone other than Oracle R&D might need to add software to an Oracle application as shown in Figure 5.6.

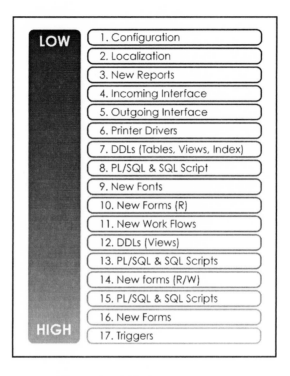

Figure 5.6 CEMLI Framework

The 17 classes are unique to Oracle applications. You should take away a few ideas from this. First, these classes, for the first time, allowed for a precise conversation. "CEMLIs" can be counted, grouped, and discussed by both the customer and Oracle—the framework eliminated the politically correct dialogue that preceded it. Second, not all CEMLIs were created equal. Adding a new report is far less invasive than adding a trigger. The classes were ranked by the level of "toxicity", meaning the likelihood that a bug in this class of software would cause data corruption or a down system. The higher the degree of toxicity, the closer you are to making fundamental modifications to the software, something you want to avoid at all costs. Finally, the CEMLI framework created an environment where the degree of customization became a business decision, not a technical or religious one. By isolating CEMLIs and separately pricing the management of these, the customer can choose how much it wants to spend for what degree of uniqueness. There were cases at Oracle where the cost to manage the CEMLIs was larger than managing the entire Oracle application.

Fred Magner, former CIO of Unocal, used the cost to manage CEMLIs to move the number of CEMLIs down from 1500 to 300 over the period of 18 months. The model created a framework for the business to justify why the particular CEMLI was worth the extra expense. So now the CIO could ask the business, "Do you want to spend X for the uniqueness, or can we use the standard product and save money?" This is no different than in the real world, where standard products, like Toyota Corollas cost far less and are more reliable than custom crafted cars like a McLaren F1. The cost for servicing the "one" is many times more than the cost of servicing the "many."

Anyone in enterprise software has faced these challenges. Taleo has addressed the customization challenge by creating a single line of code for all customers while baking in the ability for customers to do extreme configurations. This approach provides customers the ability to avoid the customization version lock trap while still enabling customers to meet their unique business requirements. Taleo CEO Michael Gregoire said, "This approach did result in us having to pass on some very large opportunities in our formative years when prospects insisted on a customized approach. However, years later, our approach has been validated, when some of these very same prospects have returned to look at Taleo to replace those same customized solutions purchased earlier from other vendors."

Concur's Michael Hilton sees the investment in architecting a solution as one reason traditional R&D and consulting are now connected. Concur created a model that allows it to easily move customizations into core code. He said, "It's just part of our development model. When you think about traditional enterprise software companies, a lot of times the teams that write customizations (typically consultants in the field) are completely separate from the core R&D teams. In our model, that doesn't work. Both teams need to be working in the same organization, utilizing the same tools and processes, so that everything scales, migrates, and works together seamlessly. At Concur, we built out a fairly complex architecture to deal with customizations. It took us a couple of years to really get it right, but the benefits are extraordinary. Our large clients can have their unique needs meet, while still operating in our multi-tenant environment."

Traditional vs. Cloud Development

But, let's get back to R&D. Perhaps no one is better qualified to talk about the differences between the traditional development and development in Model Six than Evan Goldberg. He speaks from an excellent vantage point, having spent eight years with Oracle, followed by ten years with NetSuite, as Founder, Chairman, and CTO.

In a lecture at Stanford University, Goldberg pointed out there are numerous product design benefits to Model Six. First, it is much easier to talk to the customers. As you're delivering the service, there is no "middleman" between the producer of the software and the consumer. What's more, since the software can be instrumented, you can tell what features are being used, what features aren't. Amazon.com takes special advantage of designing an operational environment that allows it to experiment with new features and, at the same time, compare with the old system. They can use data to determine what features to keep and what to retire. And, because there can be universal adoption of innovations, as a designer, you can build on top of previous innovations rather than worry about which customer has which features.

The immediate feedback loop afforded by the model allows the software engineers to, as Goldberg put it, "Kill Bugs Dead!" There is instant gratification to solving complex problems, versus the traditional model, where it may be months before a particular patch can make it into a production system. With an ability to focus on single version, software engineers can put all of their energies into that release, versus working on back porting to multiple releases on multiple platforms. Finally, given that installation is occurring on the companies' computers, the engineering staff doesn't need to spend a lot of time on simplifying installation, something, Goldberg said, "they were never good at."

The last group Goldberg addressed in his Stanford lecture was the QA organization. As we've already pointed out, delivering software as a cloud service allows for testing through actual customer usage. The ability to monitor real-time performance and develop and inventory tests based on actual usage are significant advantages over the traditional model. The challenge that QA shares with the other disciplines is that each release of software is happening much more quickly. In the case of NetSuite, the average has been over three releases per year. With such a rapid rate of change, we can't depend solely on human power so all aspects of engineering are going to have to automate.

Goldberg ended his comments by putting up a slide that said: "Operations: Welcome to the New World." He noted that, for a VP of R&D in a traditional software company, worrying about the operations of your software was a distant issue. There was always the support organization and the customers own operational people that stood between you and any issue. But in any of Models Four through Seven, that idea is a distant memory.

Summary

We've attempted to highlight some of the more important differences between traditional software development and the new world of developing software for cloud deployment. Whether it's database architecture, how you architect for customization, or how you're going to have to re-think testing and software release, it's a new world.

In our next chapter, we'll spend time on the key success factors in the management and operations of software. As Evan says, "As the VP of R&D, you're going to need to understand how to manage the security, performance, problems, change and, perhaps most importantly, the availability of your software."

SMOOTH OPERATOR

Repeat after me, *the key to excellence in anything is specialization and repetition.* This is true for all human endeavors. Swimmers swim thousands of laps to perfect a stroke, a student recites multiplication tables to learn to multiply, and a great surgeon performs hundreds of surgeries to master her craft. This is no different in the world of managing software applications. Today, an application cloud service provider manages hundreds of systems and therefore has to repeat numerous processes multiple times. Don Haig, vice president for Oracle, cites an example of repetition ultimately helping the users of Oracle applications: "Take software updates, an event that most organizations have to manage with some frequency and yet is an annoying distraction from their core business. CIOs really don't like to do updates, but understand they need to stay current on the latest release of a vendor's software. When a customer is managing their own systems, they will do this upgrade once and only once. In Oracle On Demand, upgrades have been repeated hundreds of times per year."

Upon hearing this example, Navy Captain Brian Kelly, CIO, TRICARE Military Health Services, who was trained as a neurosurgeon, said, "You don't need to explain this further. We have an expression in my business—'You don't want to be the first guy to get your cabbage worked on'." In most IT departments today, complex surgeries are done for the first time by people who read the book the night before.

Consider the following research in the medical profession in light of the complexities of managing IT infrastructure. A simple question posed to surgeons, the research shows, can often separate the talented from the average: How often do you do this? It is well known that busy hospitals generally deliver better care. But recent work adds more detail, citing the specific risks patients face in the hands of low-volume surgeons, who don't frequently and regularly perform certain procedures. "It is now a very legitimate question to ask a surgeon: How much experience with a procedure do you have? What are your complication rates?" Tufts Medical Center's surgeon-in-chief, Dr. William Mackey said. "It's something every surgeon should keep track of and show patients if requested." Do we ask the same of our operations staff? How many times have the operations staff upgraded from Release 1 to Release 2?

Some surgeons say that measuring patient volume alone is too crude a measure for grading surgeons. Increasingly, however, the profession sees constant repetition as key to mastering complex surgeries. "The more often I do a procedure, the more I fall into a standard routine," said Mackey, a vascular surgeon who performs frequent carotid endarterectomies, a delicate procedure to clear a key artery of blockages. "Then, if I encounter something out of the ordinary, I'm quicker to recognize it and correct it." Many studies of recovery from computer outages show the outage is often extended because it's the first time an operator has seen a particular issue.

So what's a high degree of repetition? Dr. Mark S. Litwin, a University of California at Los Angeles urology professor, authored a study where high volume meant 40 or more procedures annually. Consider a corporation's system, network, and database and application operations teams. How many times a week have they performed a particular procedure? Is the procedure even written down? Can it be repeated?

The good news is that if a process can be repeated 100s of times it can be automated. And computers are far better and lower cost than people. If we know the performance management process, or the upgrade process, and we've repeated it a hundred times, then why not program computers to automate the process?

To better understand what it means to automate key processes consider a simpler problem. If you went bowling ten years ago, rest assured, the first question, after "Where do I get a beer?" was likely, "Who's going to keep score? Who knows how to score?" You can be certain the same conversation was occurring in all ten bowling lanes, each with a different answer to the question. So, while all ten lanes were bowling, did a score of 200 on Lane 1 compare to a 180 on Lane 2? It was anyone's guess, since scoring was left to whoever said they remembered how. Ten years later, the story is quite different. Now, if you go into a high-tech bowling alley, or play Wii Bowling, you enter your name, and the computers score and tell you whether you get to bowl again. You can be guaranteed that a score of 200 in Lane 2 and a score of 180 in Lane 3 are scored identically. It might not improve your bowling, but you can make sure that the scoring process is being implemented consistently. Consistency and standardization are being enforced through automation.

In the remainder of this chapter, we'll go through some key processes in security, availability, performance, and problem and change management the VP of Operations, or VP of R&D will need to focus on.

The Quick Change Artist

One of the advantages of Models Four through Seven is the increased simplicity of moving customers forward to the latest release. From an R&D point of view, this is good, since your developers can focus on one code thread versus being forced to pay attention to multiple threads and platforms. And from the customer's point of view, they get to receive the benefit of new R&D, versus putting it on the shelf and avoiding the upgrade at all cost.

We should also note that upgrades or changes to enterprise business software have always been an expensive and difficult proposition. Two Northern Illinois professors documented[22] the cost and challenges of upgrading Enterprise Resource Planning (ERP) applications. Factors that range from weak project

---

[22]ERP II: best practices for successfully implementing an ERP upgrade. Communications of the ACM, 2006, Volume 49, Number 3, pages 105-109.

leadership to minimal employee product training have resulted in many ERP projects being delivered late and over budget, with costs on average 25 percent over their original budgeted amount[23]. The cost of a typical ERP implementation in a Fortune 500 company was estimated as between $40M and $240M, according to AMR Research.

Change management for applications, platform and system software sits at the nexus of the cost and reliability of delivering applications as a cloud service: there may be no more important process. Consider these four fundamental principles when designing your process:

1. Limit the locus of change
2. Standardize the frequency of change
3. Architect the software for change (roll-in & roll-back)
4. Instrument the environment.

And for the key process From-Software–Change-Initiated-Until-Completed measure the duration in minutes. As you are able to improve the predictability and improve the speed you'll not only reduce cost, but also increase the reliability.

---

[23]Peterson, W.J., Gelman, L., and Cooke, D.P. ERP Trends. The Conference Board Report, 2001.

eBay Story

If information moves along an information superhighway, then Lynn Reedy is a master traffic engineer. As the Senior VP of Product, Development and Architecture at eBay, Reedy led the group that was responsible for all of the initiatives that pertained to the company's work in software development, product specification, user interface design, usability testing, architecture and release management.

Reedy has some good counsel for anyone building software that is delivered on demand. First, she says to insure a high availability application; don't engineer for one big box, instead componentize the application so you can deploy on lots of little boxes. Furthermore, make sure you're not dependent on one large database but find a way to segment and componentize.

eBay architected a system that was based on the idea that 100 percent of the code base was sent to all of the pools of resources. A pool is a set of computers dedicated to a particular function. For example, there is a "sell your item" pool and a "My eBay" pool. The pooling architecture allowed change to be made gradually. Even within a pool, a new feature would be added to one box, then 25 percent of the pool and finally 100 percent of the pool.

eBay architected the system for change. And remember, when you make a change, you need to do this while maintaining availability of the service. As a result, eBay architected the software so that code could not only be added, it could also be rolled back. Software needed to be both forward and backward compatible. As a result, all database changes resulted in fields being added. eBay's change management process was referred to as the eBay train. With the eBay Train approach, when a new feature was developed, it was released to QA. QA tested the feature for two weeks. Once it was scheduled for a train (along with other features), the feature was subject to a battery of over 100,000 regression tests.

For large projects, the new threads were forced to merge and, thereby, pick up the changes every two or three weeks, with new software headed out on the next train. This put the impetus on the new development to resolve problems or conflicts with features coming from other organizations.

eBay knew that just depending on the quality of people and process for high productivity and reliability would not be enough. As a result, the company invested in numerous pieces of infrastructure software. At the top of the list was the central application logging (CAL) facility. CAL is both software and an engineering practice to fully instrument the application. Any exception within the system would show up as an error on the CAL graphical user interface (GUI). These components would be seen as a "red pool." Exceptions could be in the code, network, or data layer. Before CAL, eBay personnel took weeks to understand why a component "threw an exception." With CAL, resolution took minutes.

eBay's second major investment was in automated rollout and rollback. With over 200 features being worked on at any one time, and with an average of 15 features per train, eBay's usage of automated rollout and rollback were critical. Running a system that requires 7x24x365 availability, even in the event of earthquakes, tornadoes, or hurricanes is a day-one requirement. As a result eBay maintains at least three data centers in the United States. Some people have deployed fail-over sites that run "dark" and wonder, in the event of a failure, if the systems and processes could handle the failover. Instead, eBay runs every site hot and limits each site to no more than two-thirds of the overall traffic.

Reedy offers three things that every VP of Operations and R&D should focus on: right culture, right processes, and right metrics. Right culture means a culture of people who find a way to "take the hill," who think of ways to succeed, not fail. Right process means having a daily, repeatable process that everyone can do over and over again—what works for surgeons should work for IT. And finally, right metrics. Metrics tell you where you are and where you want to be. Making this as obvious to the operations team as earnings per share was to the business unit led to a standard of excellence—few can argue with Reedy's success.

You Can Never be Too Available

Most people consider the most reliable, available system in the world to be the U.S. telephone system. We often refer to "Dial-tone" reliability to describe the highest level of availability. On April 6, 1992, the FCC required telephone service providers to begin reporting outages of 30 minutes or more, which potentially affected 50,000 customers. Recently the standard has been raised to report outages affecting 30,000 customers as well as outages affecting major airports, 911, nuclear power plants, major military installations and key government facilities, regardless of the number of customers/lines affected.

The results may surprise you. For the past ten years the data has been collected. A summary of the last ten years follows.

Year	Total number of outages	Mean time between outages	Median duration of outages
1993	157	2.32 days	2.56 hours
1994	160	2.28 days	2.5 hours
1995	169	2.16 days	3.72 hours
1996	174	2.10 days	2.93 hours
1997	185	1.97 days	3.38 hours
1998	181	2.02 days	2.98 hours
1999	176	2.07 days	2.62 hours
2000	184	1.99 days	2.32 hours
2001	154	2.37 days	3.06 hours
2002	117	3.12 days	3.42 hours
10-year Average	166	2.24 days	2.94 hours

Figure 6.1 Outage Profile

These outages were caused by everything from Heisenbugs to human error to heavy rain. In Jim Gray's landmark paper,[24] he analyzed a set of Tandem NonStop systems and determined that the reasons why systems stopped fell into four large categories, with operator/human error being the majority. In a more recent study[25] of more than 500 component failures and dozens of user-visible failures in three large-scale Internet services, it was

---

[24] Why do computers stop, and what can be done about it? Tandem Technical Report TR-85.7 *www.hpl.hp.com/techreports/tandem/TR-85.7.pdf*
[25] Why do Internet services fail, and what can be done about it? David Oppenheimer, Archana Ganapathi, and David A. Patterson; University of California at Berkeley, EECS Computer Science Division, Berkeley, CA, http://roc.cs.berkeley.edu/papers/usits03.pdf

observed that (1) operator error was the leading cause of failure in two of the three services studied, (2) operator error was the largest contributor to time to repair in two of the three services, and (3) configuration errors were the largest category of operator errors. Operators may face such difficulties because computer designers and programmers have frequently sacrificed ease of use in the quest for better performance. Database software, for example, can require a full-time staff of trained administrators to manage it. Ironically, because hardware and software have grown cheaper over time, operator salaries are now often the biggest expense in running complex Internet sites.

The experience in the field leads to forming a handful of fundamental principles in availability management:

1. Develop a high speed, predictable recovery process: problems are going to happen, so design systems that recover quickly.
2. Instrument to pinpoint the sources of faults
3. Build systems that support an "undo" function, so operators can correct their mistakes.
4. Standardize the key management processes and take operations people out of the loop

In the end the key availability management process, From-The-Time-The-Failure-Is-Detected-Until-The-Time-The Application-Is-Live, is perhaps the most important. Furthermore as the recovery time is made predictable and reduced not only will you have happier customers, but the cost of providing high reliability will go down.

It's About the Performance

Your customers expect you to provide them with application access at an acceptable level of performance. Performance and availability management are related. If you expect a result in 2 seconds and it takes 200 seconds, does it really matter if the application is slow or down. Performance management starts with the difficult task of workload characterization. Every application has key queries, transaction flows, searches, etc. that characterize that application. Once identified, these workload characteristics can be monitored. Perhaps the most famous one you see every day is in the upper right hand corner of every Google Query.

View customizations

Results 1 - 10 of about **32,500,000** for **cloud computing**. (**0.22** seconds)

Detecting a slow application is now an exercise in profiling the performance of the application, then seeing when the application is performing outside of those norms. One company totally dedicated to this is Keynote, it allows you to monitor the performance of your web application from points around the globe. Of course, once you detect a slow application then you're back to using the change management processes we discussed earlier in the chapter.

Batten Down the Hatches

Before enterprises can reap the benefits of on-demand software, providers will have to convince IT managers and CIOs that the services they offer are reliable and, perhaps more important, secure. For many, the push to put information in the cloud raises the specter of information breaches. While a discussion about securing online applications could take the remainder of the book, we're going to highlight a couple of specific areas you'll need to think about to insure the applications are secure.

- Authentication. Whether thru simple password management, all the way up to two-factor authentication with retinal eye scan all security mechanisms begin with knowing who you are – authentically.

- Authorization. Authorization mechanisms ensure authenticated individuals have access to authorized data per a security policy. The simpler the definition of the security policy and the clear evidence that it is implemented insure the highest degree of trust.

- Audit. At the core of all security management is auditing. Audit considerations include the process to access audit logs, retention durations and evidence of tamper proofing.

- Encryption. When physical data protection offered by the datacenter facility is not possible (e.g., on a tape, removable disk, network) encryption becomes the service of choice. Encyrption also solves problems of protection when data leaves one application domain and enters another (e.g., PIN encryption).

In the security management area there are numerous standards. One of the most recognized commercial standards is the Statement on Auditing Standards No. 70 (SAS 70). A SAS 70 audit is performed by an independent auditor and results in a SAS 70 report. One should be mindful that a SAS 70 report only documents the internal control practices of an organization, without offering any judgment as to whether they are satisfactory. Due diligence therefore requires that you not only request an SAS 70 report from a prospective provider, but that you examine it thoroughly to determine whether the provider is able to comply with your own internal standards for privacy, data security, and so on.

Care Rehab Story

"For Care Rehab, a medical device manufacturer, security was an important consideration when the company was evaluating Salesforce.com," said Ed Barrett, vice president at the 200-person company. The company, which makes traction and electrotherapy devices used by physical therapy clinics, has been using Salesforce.com's software to monitor the activities of its salespeople and to track its entire inventory, as devices are prescribed by doctors and dispensed to patients. Care Rehab audited Salesforce.com's security practices before agreeing to use the software. That audit included Salesforce.com staff members showing Care Rehab how they secured the data that was stored on their servers and reading documents describing Salesforce.com's security practices. "Their security is superior to what we provide for ourselves," said Barrett. "If you're Salesforce.com, you have to have the best people in security and the best redundancies. [We] need to have the best salespeople. I'm sure we aren't the world's best security people."

Mexico Story

We'll end this section with one personal story. A few years ago, I had the opportunity to speak with the Secretary of Treasury of Mexico. In my introductory remarks, I made a point to tell the Secretary we could implement the Oracle On Demand model either in an Oracle data center in Austin, Texas, or a data center of his choice, presumably in Mexico City. I spoke for about ten minutes and then asked him if he had any questions. He said, "Tell me about your security." I, of course, went through all the security features from the data center, through encrypted VPNs, through SAS 70 Level II audits. But I ended my answer by sharing a conversation I'd had the previous week with the CIO of OCBC Bank, one of the largest banks in Singapore. In that situation, mid-way into my explaining the breadth of on demand services the CIO said, "I want you to take my HR and Payroll data." I, of course, said yes, but asked him why was he so adamant. He replied, "I know my DBAs can see their salaries, their bosses' salaries and their bosses' bosses' salaries. I know your folks can see the same information, but what would it mean to them?"

It's a perfect story to end with, since security professionals agree that most IT-related attacks arise within the organization.

According to security professional Michael Bruck[26], four-fifths of all IT-related attacks arise within the organization. Bruck's estimate is consistent with a survey[27] of more than 200 IT professionals, which found one-third of them admitting to abusing their administrative access privileges to examine sensitive data unrelated to their job functions. About one-fourth reported knowledge of former employees who retained access to sensitive networks long after their termination, with one-third stating a belief that they could do likewise with little risk of detection.

Customer Service

While many think of customer service management as defect management, with any software that has a reasonable degree of maturity, the challenge of customer service management is not around defects—it's around delivering information, personal to you. Just to drive the point home in 2004, Oracle's Support group received one hundred million requests for service. Now, most people would think one hundred million requests would be for software patches to fix defects. The analysis was quite the opposite. Just one-tenth of one percent (0.1 percent) of the requests actually resulted in any new software fixes; ninety-nine point nine percent (99.9 percent) could be answered by

---

[26]Bruck, Michael. Security Threats from Within. Entrepreneur.com, June 28, 2007.
[27]Survey Reveals Scandal of Snooping IT Staff. Cyber-Ark Software Inc. Press release. May 30, 2007.

knowledge in a library, existing patches that were contained in a patch distribution system or in people's heads—in short, known information. So if you've ever been on hold with a call center in the post-Google era, haven't you wondered why the information was so difficult to find?

Search-based Applications

Today's surface Web (which Google, Yahoo and others have indexed) is thought to contain ten billion pages; or somewhere on the order of 25-50 terabytes of information. But this surface Web of less than 100 terabytes pales in comparison to the deep Web of information contained in every business. How deep is it? Consider that 1,030 *peta*bytes (a petabyte is 1,000 terabytes) of hard disk capacity was shipped in the fourth quarter of 2006. The simple math says the deep Web is, at a minimum, 10,000 times the size of the surface Web. Sales, support, HR, purchasing, and manufacturing information are all locked up in relational databases, document management systems, and file systems all around the world. While seeing or indexing the information is one thing, the challenge is finding the relevant information.

The opportunity to mine this deep Web has not been lost on numerous companies. Google launched their Enterprise

Appliance in 2002 and, every year since, has produced a major new release. Today they are deployed in over 9,000 sites around the world. Independent companies like Fast, which was acquired by Microsoft for over $1B, and Autonomy, the second highest valued European software company after SAP, have both focused on the challenges of enterprise search.

While these efforts have all been successful, enterprise search in 2009 is today probably only a $500M business. This is small when compared to the SQL database business, which today probably exceeds $10B annually. So why the gap? Perhaps the answer lies in tracing the history of SQL. Oracle was the most successful at commercializing SQL and by 1987 was generating $100M a year. Relational database technology, however, has no intrinsic business value (it's just cool technology). It took the advent of enterprise SQL-based applications like Remedy, Peoplesoft, SAP, Siebel, and many more to make the technology useful to business.

If the pattern is to repeat itself, we need to understand what it means to have search-based applications. John Lervick, who founded FAST, said "Google has been good and bad for search. Good because they made search important; bad because they've made everyone think it's a search bar. Search can be so much more if you think of it as a technology platform." So what might these search-based applications look like?

Udi Manber, who has been Chief Scientist at Yahoo, Chief Algorithms Officer at Amazon.com, and was lured away a few years ago to be VP of Engineering at Google, once described the Internet in a very interesting way. He said searching the Internet is like taking all the books out of the Library of Congress, ripping all of the pages out, throwing them on the floor and using a search bar to try and read them. If you think about it, he's basically right, and trying to read a book through a search bar makes little sense. He recently unveiled a project called Knol. Knol pages are "meant to be the first thing someone who searches for this topic for the first time will want to read," according to Manber. The term knol means a "unit of knowledge," and has been seen by many as Google's attempt to compete with Wikipedia.

While Knol is targeted at the consumer Internet, a new company, Openwater Networks, has engineered a search-based application cloud service. Michael Rocha, co-founder and CEO of Openwater Networks, was previously the EVP for Oracle's $5B+ product support and services business. In that capacity, he saw how the customers of complex applications struggled with being able to understand their software, their business processes, and their environments. While 99.9 percent of all their service requests were met with known information, it was the cost and difficulty of delivering that information that inspired him to bring modern Internet technology to the problem.

The search-based application fundamentally does three things. First, it standardizes the language (much as SQL-based applications have standardized processes) of a group, a team, or a business unit. Second, the application is read and write. While this has been a characteristic of all SQL-based apps few people think of search-based applications as having this capability. Finally, the search-based application acknowledges that people add value to the information, as opposed to traditional SQL-based applications, which only control which people have access to which information.

It will take a new generation of these kinds of search-based applications to truly use the information buried in the Deep Web. But with greater and greater access to search technology, whether in open source or in the cloud, there are bound to be hundreds of search-based applications just as there are hundreds of SQL-based apps.

Summary

Of all of the major functional areas, managing operations is the most foreign to a traditional software company. But having a system of repetitive, automatable operations is the key to low-cost and high-quality customer experiences. This chapter has highlighted some of the areas in the management of change, problems, availability, security and performance. We've now walked thru each layer of the cloud stack and now will focus the remaining chapters on the important areas for anyone building next generation application cloud services. How will you market the application, sell the service, finance and organize yourself for success?

7

WHO'S IN THE ELEVATOR?

So let's assume you've built the world's coolest application and it's going to revolutionize poultry management, or just the next major release of your ERP application. How is anyone going to know? Once upon a time you'd hire an "ad man" who would come up with an ad campaign and then find out if you could afford to run it in the Wall Street Journal, or just the Palo Alto Weekly. You'd have to make sure your tagline was short and sweet since you had no idea who would read it. As a result many people think marketing means coming up with a clever tagline and finding a way to make it into a Super Bowl ad. This might have made sense when the production and distribution of information was expensive, but with the advent of the Internet and rich media, we clearly no longer need to think this way. In this chapter we'll focus on marketing your product. We'll discuss the fundamental economics, the traditional approaches and some of the newer ways for you to educate the buyers.

Economics of Sales & Marketing

We'll begin by considering the Webex case study by becoming students of their P&L shown in Figure 7.1. The funding line shows each round of funding they raised, which totaled $107M prior to their IPO in 2002. You can also see that, in 1996 and 1997, they operated at or near profitability. In these early years, Min and Subrah financed their operations by having a group of low cost engineers implement software and plowing the profits back into funding WebEx (at the time called Active Touch). This approach resulted in both founders maintaining significant ownership of the company. You'll notice the explosive growth from 2000 to 2001. This was the by-product of both a significant investment in sales and marketing and the explosive growth of Web conferencing post September 11. You should note that Webex's spend in sales and marketing is hovering around 35 percent, the single largest line item. Consider the implication of this, given how we all view Web conferencing as simple to use and simple to explain and simple to buy.

WEBEX	1996	1997	1998	1999	2000	2001	2002	2003	2004
Funding			$7M	$25M	$75M		IPO		
Net Revenue	$481	$1,289	$1,987	$2,607	$25,389	$81,186	$139,861	$189,341	$249,133
Cost of Revenue	$38	$192	$484	$688	$10,061	$21,527	$25,064	$31,798	$41,854
Gross Profit	$443	$1,097	$1,503	$1,919	$15,308	$59,659	$114,797	$157,543	$207,279
Sales & Marketing	$103	$421	$2,244	$9,319	$50,807	$47,207	$58,026	$74,249	$84,192
R&D	$713	$525	$1,406	$3,361	$12,168	$16,284	$22,788	$24,769	$34,342
G&A	$48	$125	$198	$1,732	$6,553	$10,301	$14,447	$13,575	$18,713
Equity Based Compensation			$92	$2,005	$28,039	$13,668	$2,966	$1,849	$571
Total Operating Expenses	$864	$1,071	$3,940	$16,417	$97,567	$87,460	$98,227	$114,442	$137,818
Operating Income	-$421	-326	-$2,437	$14,498	-$82,259	$16,570	$16,570	$43,101	$69,461

Figure 7.1 WebEx P&L

Traditional Sales & Marketing

For those of you who have been doing high tech sales and marketing this section will be old hat. Traditional marketing and sales has broken the pipeline into a series of stages.

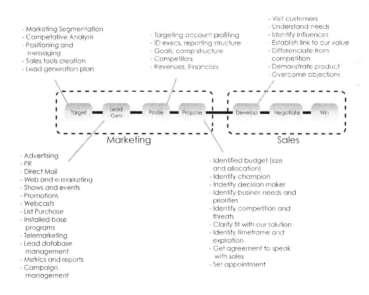

Figure 7.2 Traditional Sales & Marketing Pipeline

Early stages of the pipeline focus on getting awareness, then leads. Leads are both nurtured and qualified ultimately transitioning from a centralized marketing organization to the field where the potential customer is engaged. Ultimately, the big difference between consumer and enterprise sales and marketing is that there is not one decision maker – enterprise sales and marketing of imprecise, more expensive things is a team sport. Consider Figure 7.3 and talk to anybody selling business software. Even with a highly qualified lead the sales person finds himself or herself in the roll of traffic cop (or switchboard operator). Different constituencies within the buying enterprise have questions that can only be answered by members of the selling enterprise (or customers that have already purchased – the reference customer). Scheduling the phone calls, lunches, and web conferences is time consuming and further elongates the sales process. No news here for any of you who've sold enterprise technology.

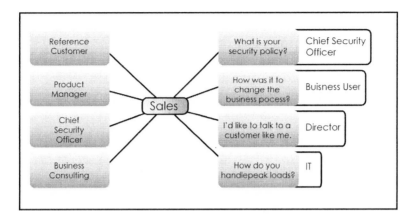

Figure 7.3 Sales is a Team Sport

Hopefully thru CRM applications this process can be made more efficient, repetitive and specialized. We'll focus on a few areas where marketing services have developed to improve sales productivity.

Email Marketing

Email marketing, as an alternative to direct mail, has been an area of considerable growth. This is largely because the economics are so compelling. Emailing to a list of 1,000 people costs $5 versus over $500 to send out direct mail. Companies like Constant Contact, Lyris, Responsys have specialized in this area. As a specialist they focus on the details. Everything from the number of characters in the subject line (keep to less than 50) to the time the email is sent out can determine the effectiveness.

Day	Time	Open Rate
Tuesday / Wednesday	11:30am - 11:30pm	50-52%
Thursday	3:30pm	34-44%
Friday	9:30am	16%

Figure 7.4 Call at the right time

e-Loan Story

Scott Hilson, Director, Customer Services at Responsys, has helped many companies implement successful email marketing campaigns. As a simple case study, Siara Nazir, Director of Online/Offline marketing at E-LOAN, implemented an email program designed to remind and encourage prospective borrowers to complete their mortgage applications. The program involves integration with the E-LOAN Web site to identify prospects that started but failed to complete the mortgage application. It was executed in two phases. The first phase, triggered 30 minutes after the application was abandoned, reminded applicants to complete the process, provided a quick link to the partially completed application, and encouraged applicants to use phone support. The second phase, sent one week later, called the applicant's attention to the company's value proposition and also offered a quick link to the incomplete application. Built into the program was the ability to perform A/B testing on the messages sent to the customers. As a result of this campaign, 32% more applications were completed by the control group that abandoned but did get the automated follow up email.

Search Marketing

A company's Web site has become the face of the company so improving the volume and quality of traffic to a Web site from search engines via search results is clearly important. While there is plenty of advice on how to spend money on ad words, we all know we click on natural search results more often than the ads on the side. By paying attention to how Web pages are built and the content put in them, you can create natural search results that drive traffic to your site without purchasing advertising (and more importantly be significantly more effective). Katy Roth, who after years of experience in marketing Model Six companies formed her own consultancy, has some fundamental advice for anyone trying to optimize natural search results.

- Build a FAQ into your Web site to capitalize on potential customers searching for reference or problem solving information. This way, you become the expert on the technology and the problem your company is trying to solve. For example, Solarwinds, a network management company, saw a lot of traffic coming to their site because of their extensive network management content.

- Blogs are great for generating traffic. The content is generally considered by search engines to be fresher and more authentic, giving it higher weight in the results.

FiveRuns, a provider of monitoring and development products for Ruby on Rails, developed content on their blog that provided answers and guidance to Rails developers. See the previous section on blogging.

- Have your community create content. iTaggit.com is a good example of a company that reworked their forms to pull in more community generated content. But they didn't stop there. They worked with their developers to tune their page generation engine to produce better meta-information that allowed their pages to come up to the top of natural search results.

- Work with a search engine savvy developer to make sure the meta content of your Web pages is optimized. There is nothing worse than seeing a page with terrific content with a generic browser title. Just check out Wikipedia for some good examples.

Social Media Marketing

Facebook's early success with college aged people has caused some people to see social networks as just a tool to hook up or find old friends. But Facebook has become much more. The number of users has grown from 60M users in 2008 to over 300M with the fastest growing demographic being people 35-55. Since Februrary 2009, Facebook leads Google, Yahoo and MySpace in total time spent online by Americans (6% of total time). Twitter has also enjoyed phenomenal growth growing 1,300% this year. Today more than 15 million users create 1,500 "Tweets" every second.

WHO'S IN THE ELEVATOR?

Perhaps the best way to think about Facebook and Twitter is as a next generation telephone – and a very powerful telephone. As an example consider the recent case where Facebook simultaneously broadcast a soccer match in Spain for the Spanish Facebook community. Within 30 minutes of the game starting the video servers crashed. Why? Because once one person commented and his social graph saw the comment (and started watching the game) and another friend commented and another, there were suddenly 100s of thousands of viewers. Think of doing the same thing with a telephone and you'll begin to understand the potential of these social networks.

The application of these social networks to sales and marketing is still in its infancy. Clara Shih attended the first Facebook developer conference in 2007. With her friend Todd Perry's help, she developed Faceconnector which pulls Facebook profile and friend information into salesforce.com. Now instead of anonymous cold calling, sales reps could get to know the person behind the name and title, and even ask for warm introductions from mutual friends.

Clara's counsel[28] for those thinking about using social networking in your marketing efforts:

---

[28] The Facebook Era: Tap Online Social Networks to Build Better Products, Reach More People, and Sell More Stuff, Claire Shih

- Use hyper targeting as an opportunity to test new audiences and see if your product can gain traction. Prior to hyper targeting, it was often cost-prohibitive to do this in any systematic way.

- Use the social graph and knowledge about relationships across your audience to create a more personalized online community.

- Think about using social networks to market yourself as an individual. Your profile information, photos, and friends all paint a picture of who you are and help to establish your brand.

Get Notorious

This brings us to getting notorious. Once upon a time the product marketing person interviewed the developers of the product, spent weeks writing up a data sheet, deciding the colors, quantity, and quality of the print that ultimately made it into a folder at an event at the Hyatt in San Francisco. But there are many more sources of information. You have internal experts on the product in customer support, sales, R&D, product management, field service, and consulting. Not only are your people sources of information, but so too are your customers. Customers of your product (the valued reference customers) that you metered out onto a conference call with a carefully selected sales person and prospect today can have their testimonials videoed and made available on YouTube.

WHO'S IN THE ELEVATOR?

While the old world of low bandwidth, expensive communication required that you needed to aggregate content in the Internet behind the veil of "the company" today we should be able to know what you think, what you believe, and what you can contribute. As you develop your marketing programs, think about whom in your company, in your customers, in your third parties, should become notorious. Encourage them to write, or speak, or do Webinars or videos and communicate their expertise and more importantly their point of view. By bringing more contributors into your marketing cloud, we will be able to find the knowledge we need delivered the way we want it—in a language and context that is accessible to each of us.

A few bloggers including Vinnie Mirchandani, Anshu Sharma, Charlie Wood, and Ed Herrmann provide some advice on getting notorious.

- Be notorious - Don't send a note from "your company." Reach out as an individual Name, title, and phone number. Blogging is personal.

- Use video - but not an overproduced one. No talking heads-show the product. Limit it to 30 seconds. Make me think: "Wow, that's impressive!"

- Check out Digg - Look at the first few pages. See what formats are popular, and use those. (Top 10's, video, photo essays, controversy, "best ever's, generally "this is so cool!").

Educate & Select

Sales and marketing have been critical components of traditional software companies and new software companies. Perhaps the greatest change is, as we move closer to delivering these applications as a cloud service, as they become more specialized, and as the price point goes down, we must re-invent the traditional account management model, the traditional human network that has powered sales for the last twenty-five years.

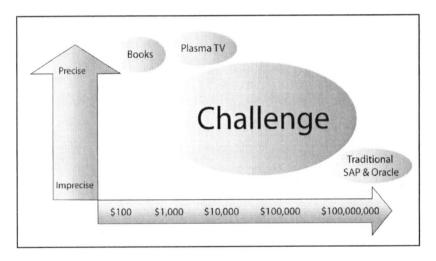

Figure 7.5 Selling Spectrum

As you begin to tackle this problem, consider the fact that, last Christmas, very few people were sold a plasma TV. We're not saying there weren't a lot bought, just that they were not bought because of a sales person. Consider Figure 7.5. As a technology industry, we have figured out how to sell expensive items ($1M) that are not very precise (SAP Manufacturing) and have grown large profitable businesses. We have also figured out how to sell low price (<$100), precise items. You only have to look at Amazon or eBay to see how successful this model has been. Our challenge is how we effectively sell imprecise items that cost $10,000.

We should take a lesson from the Plasma TV. The reason no sales person sold a TV is that most consumers of Plasma TVs did their research online; they figured out the right size screen, read what others thought about the TV and, by the time they were ready to purchase, had made their selection. Purchasing became a transaction. Perhaps this is what can happen in the future market for software. People will educate themselves on the good and bad of the solution, talk to experts and other users and, in the end, select the right answer for themselves. Selling may be replaced by education and selection.

Summary

The Internet changes everything used to be a corporate tagline. Perhaps it is no more obvious than in the art and science of marketing. With a low cost means of delivering notorious content, you now have an ability to deliver personalized information to every member of the team that influences a purchasing decision—when they want it, in the way they want it.

While communicating to people, whether they find you through search, email, or social networks, you still need marketing. In the end, no matter how simple we try to make the software, the act of matching what a potential customer needs and what you have to offer remains the role of a quality marketing organization.

HANNIBAL THE CANNIBAL

While SaaS or cloud computing might be all the rage, it doesn't take too long until someone says, "But this will cannibalize our existing sales." Sometimes it's stated even more clearly. Early in 2002, Ken Rudin, who today is the CEO of LucidEra, was asked by Tom Siebel to lead the efforts for Siebel On Demand. Rudin, of course, wasn't sure if it was a good idea, but Siebel finally convinced him. After about a year, Rudin was able to work out the product strategy and business model. There was a sense of urgency, as Salesforce.com was winning more and more business. Finally, he was ready to tackle the sales and distribution channel, and he scheduled a meeting with the head of North American sales. The VP listened politely to Rudin's presentation and, at the conclusion, said, "Ken, that's an outstanding plan, but stay the f—k away from my accounts!"

This chapter is dedicated to sales and distribution. More than with any other group, the solutions to the challenges here will make or break any new business. In Models Four and Five, you will need to figure out how to leverage your existing sales force. In Model Six, the challenges will pertain to developing a new sales force in a world where the economics don't bring you million-dollar deals that can fund the creation of a channel.

For the traditional software company, moving existing applications to delivery as a cloud service with an existing channel and product (Models Four and Model Five), your primary advantage is that you already have a sales channel. But, there are many challenges. Does it mean the comp plan will change? Is this new on-demand group going to compete with my sales force? How important is lead generation? In this chapter, we'll address some of these issues and also let you hear from some successful sales and marketing executives.

Transforming Traditional Software Sales

Every Model One software company worries about cannibalization when they consider a move to delivery of their software as a cloud service. It doesn't have to be this way. If you adopt Model Four, the existing sales force continues to sell the software as it always has. Whether that's a perpetual or term license, nothing changes. The only change is they have a new delivery option (one which they can be compensated for). Do you want to manage our software or do you want us to manage our software? Do you want to capitalize and pay for the software, hardware, third-party software, etc., up front or expense it over time?

Joe King, who led sales for Oracle On Demand for seven years and today is Group Vice-President of JDA's on demand business, has first-hand experience in how to sell when you're in Model Four. His first piece of advice is to make sure you find a team of sales professionals that have a mix of experience in selling both traditional software products and services. Next, organize the sales teams around current delivery capabilities. Ensure that the sales team is setting proper expectations with the customers and selling a solution that your company has the ability to deliver on today. Unlike selling traditional software, Joe says, "Don't sell futures!" Finally, train the sales reps to find customer challenges that can be solved by having you provide the complete solution without letting the customer dissect the solution into its components. In other words, it's important to discuss the underlying infrastructure that supports the solution, but remember the customer is not buying servers and data centers separately from your complete solution.

When you get to the CIO or IT director, who inevitably says: "I can do this" (because they have), counter that when a software company delivers the service in a repetitive standardized way, it can insure security, manage upgrades, and identify performance problems better and lower cost than a single isolated IT department can having to figure it out itself.

Selling New Application Cloud Services

A Model Six business selling software as a service is in many ways no different than selling traditional software in Model One. In other words, the software must solve a particular important business problem. What is different is the economics of the sales process. In Model Six, the average selling price will be significantly under $100,000 (for the first year), so you no longer can create a sales channel with the large up-front license fee. As a result, the traditional Model One sales person makes a good living managing a few accounts is unaffordable in the new world.

While that is worse than the old world, some things that are better. Since the software is either "always deployed", "ready to be used," or "quickly configured," scheduling custom demos is a thing of the past. With adequate Web marketing and standard demo deployment, some customers can even find and try your product.

Joe Graves, CIO at Stratus Computers, a $250M a year computer company, is a big user of application cloud services. He uses Salesforce.com, QuickArrow, Eloqua, Xactly, SpringCM, Ceridian, Halogen, WebEx, and Postini. Joe explained how different traditional software companies are from new Model Six companies. A Model One software company offered to do a free six-week discovery process, followed by a demo eight weeks later. Instead, Stratus deployed a Model Six solution in seven weeks—worldwide.

Salesforce.com and WebEx can attribute their high growth and early success to having products that could be used simply and economically by small group. That's the good news. The bad news is the average selling price is considerably lower than in either the traditional Model One, or even Model Four or Five businesses. While the specific numbers are always changing consider the ASP for salesforce.com and Webex.

Salesforce.com averages 20 seats per customer, with an average price per seat of $70 per month, so its average yearly contract is under $20,000. WebEx's high-end customers average $25,000 per year, but half of its customers have an average yearly contract of less than $1,000 per year. The point of these numbers is the average selling price is nowhere near the ASP of traditional Model One enterprise software.

A Model Six company must have volume, and when you need volume, you need a sales machine. WebEx's approach is to spend nearly $100,000 in marketing per sales rep per year. This includes free trials, daily demos (scheduled and executed from India), Webinars, and email campaigns. Every lead from this marketing is categorized into three buckets. High priority leads are responded to within 24 hours; the next level within 72 hours. It had perfected quite a sales engine, with an eight-to-one conversion ratio and a fifteen-day sales cycle.

Salesforce.com also had a few tricks up its sleeve. Aaron Ross was Director of Corporate Sales with Salesforce.com from 2001 to 2006. When asked what advice he could give for establishing high velocity sales, he said something counter-intuitive: "The size of your sales team does not drive growth." In the past sales would drive growth by hiring more sales people, who worked their patches to generate more leads and close more business. Today, that doesn't work. Ross says, hiring more sales people is not the main engine of growth. Instead, generating more leads for sales to close drives growth. Instead of obsessing over the number of sales people in your team, obsess over sales productivity. There are not enough great sales reps to hire out there, so helping your current team do more with less is as important as hiring.

Ross also said: "Give up Control." Historically, the sales organization wanted control over the sale. This was possible, because it was very difficult for customers to get unbiased information about vendors. The Internet changes that. Today, prospects can find out as much as they want about you before they call. Vendors can't control the flow of information. The best strategy is to embrace this and give the prospect as much information and control over the sales as you can. The right question is - how much can you educate the decision makers and influencers?

Ross' next suggestion also sounds counter-intuitive to old-school sales people: "Stop the 'Always be closing' mindset." Buyers already have seen all the sales tricks and programs, and anything artificial irritates them. Instead of "Always be closing," focus on building a sales team that is constantly asking,

"Are we a match?" You can't afford to waste much time (money) on prospects that aren't a great fit.

Finally, lead generation and lead qualification are as important as closing. Most sales people focus too much on the second half of the sales process: sales deals in the pipeline and which deals can close. They tend to ignore the first half of the process: lead generation and lead qualification. Yet, the more sales invests in increasing the quantity and *quality* of leads, the more high quality deals will be in the sales pipeline, making sales results easier. Common mistakes are: not hiring enough junior sales people to qualify inbound leads and not creating a *dedicated* team that do nothing but outbound prospecting. One way to fail at generating leads is to expect your own quota-carrying sales reps to do it. They are terrible at it, they hate doing it, and as soon as they get a few deals in their pipeline, they become too busy to prospect.

Contracts

Contracts vary significantly from model to model. Since the earliest forms of selling software as a service were large outsourcing deals (Model Three), Models Four through Six carry with legacy contract issues with them.

The outsourcing (Model Three) business is still growing around the world. Forrester reported companies based in Europe, the Middle East, and Africa (EMEA) signed 75 large outsourcing deals with a total value of almost €5.7B in Q1 of 2007. The contracts for those deals are probably similar to the one Bechtel's CIO, Hank Leingang, plowed through when he outsourced desktop support and network management to Electronic Data Systems: "It was three inches thick."

This degree of complexity has created a cottage industry in providing advice to companies negotiating contracts. TPI is a leading global outsourcing advisory firm. It published a paper providing advice to customers renegotiating outsourcing contracts. When asked about the duration of renegotiation, 85 percent of those surveyed indicated the restructuring process required less than a year to complete. Fifty-five percent finished renegotiations in less than six months, and 13 percent finished in less than three months.[29]

At the other end of the contract spectrum are the online click wrap agreements. The Yahoo terms of service or the WebEx contracts are good examples. Typical Model Six terms allow customers to pay on a month-to-month basis, and can be

---

[29]Restructuring Outsourcing Agreements: An Indication of Failure, or a Tool to Increase Value? TPI Report, January 2007.

terminated with 30-days notice. Some vendors require a two-year commitment others apply a percentage penalty against the total contract value if a customer cancels prematurely.

Service Level Agreements

In almost all Models Three through Six contracts SLAs (Service Level Agreements) are important. In Model Three, SLAs are heavily negotiated. If you want to spend a couple of frustrating days, you can lock five experts in a room and try to define what uptime means and what penalties you should pay if the uptime is not met. SLA requirements vary. Companies like Salesforce.com set SLAs on contractual terms on a case-by-case basis. Blackbaud On Demand, the contracts typically stipulate 99.9 percent uptime guarantee and provide specific commitments for data handling and server maintenance. "We occasionally modify the terms slightly for customer's specific needs, but it is a competitive agreement," says Blackbaud's CEO Marc Chardon. "We're very strict on ourselves, as this agreement governs what we do operationally."

Taleo provides penalties in its contract if it doesn't meet uptime standards. Although the financial penalty might seem minimal to the individual customer, uptime problems usually affect the entire customer base. Taleo's incentiveto keep the system up and running all day and every day is enormous.

The important point is that the users of your application will want the service to perform so you should first focus on the service level your operations and development group are engineering to deliver. After that, you can decide to what extent these metrics are included in a contract. As noted earlier, Oracle pioneered a different approach, simply called the "Nordstrom's guarantee." Service levels in availability, security, problem, change, and performance management were published and reported. If the customer was dissatisfied with the service for any reason, it could request a rebate of 20 percent per month - no questions asked. In four years under the Nordstrom's guarantee, fewer than a handful of rebates were paid.

The Nordstrom's guarantee separates the issue of penalties from the description of service level metrics and objectives. Writing these down and measuring them is key to improving the overall quality of the service. Here are the major areas you should focus on.

- Change Management – Define how often upgrades to new releases will occur. Will you move all customers at once, or will you stage them over a three-month period?

- Availability Management – Many contracts call out percentages of availability (99.5 percent, 99.7 percent, 99.9 percent, and 99.99 percent… They all sound about the same, don't they?). This begs the question of whether this refers to unplanned or planned outages. You should consider defining availability by total number of outage minutes per month, per quarter, per year, and do that for planned and unplanned outages. It will cause you to focus on how rapidly you recover, which is a much more important metric.

- Security Management – Have you completed a SAS 70 audit? How frequently are backups taken? Where are backups stored? How fast can data be restored? Under normal circumstances or in the case where there is complete site failure because a disaster has occurred.

- Customer service management – When a customer has a question about your software (these could be defects or just usage), what level of service will you be providing?

- Performance Management – What response time should customers expect? How much disk space is included? How quickly should reports run? This will be a difficult area, but providing some reference implementation to benchmark on a release-to-release basis will help you provide performant apps. For a service level that is reported on every transaction, just look at the upper right-hand side of your Google search results when you search for "SaaS".

You would be wise to separate the definitions of your service levels from the legal and contractual side. Become a student of WebEx's and Salesforce.com's contracts and terms. Some will push you towards EDS or IBM Global Service agreements.

Instead, be proactive about the service levels you will provide and publish them to your customers. In the end, remember the customer wants the service to work.

Sales Compensation

Marc Chardon, CEO of Blackbaud, points out the universal truth in effective sales compensation: You're looking for sales people to respond to the metrics that you give them. "We try as much as possible to make the sales rep indifferent to selling an on-demand or on-premise version," he said. "If you create a level playing field in the sales compensation, and if the solutions are roughly as easy to sell, sales reps should be, and usually are, good at evaluating the shortest time necessary to get their commission."

When you look for expertise in sales compensation you'd have to consider the team at Callidus Software. They have some guidelines that are applicable across a number of our seven business models.

- Keep your compensation plans straightforward. Many companies come up with plans with dozens of variables and multiple levels of intricate dependencies.
- Make sure you have the data—and that it's clean.
- Report regularly, transparently, and consistently with the plan type and organizational style. One good (transparent) report delivered to payees at the right

frequency keeps the focus and motivation where it should be.

- Credit directly for sales compensation. The most effective plans credit the primary seller along with those directly connected to that seller in the chain of command.

- Create a transparent dispute resolution process. Even if you are able to follow every piece of advice above, errors and problems will happen.

- Analyze and change on a predictable schedule. The smartest and most successful companies are constantly evaluating their sales performance data and are not afraid to make changes to compensation plans.

Installed Base Sales

Most of the focus on selling has been on getting the new customer, again a by-product of selling a product for large upfront money versus driving revenue on a monthly or yearly basis. While traditional sales has been on trying to know something about a customer you don't have – for the first time companies can now focus on learning more about the customer they do have and based on that information personalize the offering using that knowledge.

Nowhere is this more obvious than in the case of Amazon. But how can this be applied to higher ASP, less precise products? Here we can take a lesson out of the notebook of computer architecture. Computer architects have struggled with how to make computers faster and faster. While turning up the clock speed is one answer, another answer lies in being more efficient about how an instruction is executed. Below is a diagram showing the typical execution of an instruction. Years ago every instruction took 5 clock cycles to execute, as a result seven instructions would take 35 ticks of the clock. But over 10 years ago some smart guys figured out if you could separate instruction execution into 5 stages, 5 parts, each taking the **same** amount of time (1 tick of the clock) then instead of 35 ticks to get 7 instructions executed you could do it in 11 ticks. So with the same clock speed the computer was in the limit five times faster.

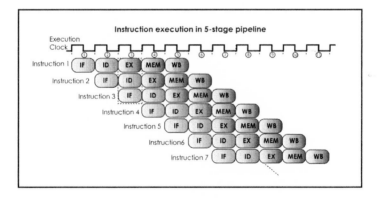

Figure 8.1 Pipelining

So what does this have to do with sales? Our marketing & sales pipeline is no different only the clock ticks are not so fast. The conventional way of managing the pipeline is no different than the traditional way of instruction execution – we finish one deal, one instruction, before we start the next. But indeed the same principles can be applied, and were applied to sell a standardized Model Four service to 10,000 companies who already owned Oracle applications. The trick is to engineer each stage of the pipeline to last a fixed period of time (e.g., 2 weeks) and then move customers from one stage of the pipeline to the next. Then each stage could be optimized and specialized and over time sales transactions could be much more parallel than they are today. Anyone selling to a large installed base so reconsider how – and not just treat it the same as potential customers – where you have no idea who they area, nor what experience they've had with the product.

Indirect Channels

The last major generation of computing was called client-server computing. Its rise was not only driven by the availability of low cost hardware (Dell, Compaq, etc.) and low cost software (Microsoft, Corel, etc.) but also by the creation of a new channel of distribution. Names like Ingram Micro, Tech Data and CDW, today all multi-billion dollar companies, provided a low cost indirect channel that matched the price of the technology products.

This client-server indirect channel has been built on delivering "boxes and bodies" to implement and deliver the application. Unfortunately, whether you're in Model Four, Model Five or Model Six, you are now in competition with these traditional channel players. In early 2006, I had the opportunity to spend a day with one of Microsoft's largest resellers for its Great Plains Software. While the reseller saw the value of a Model Six business, they were as addicted to the "perpetual license drug" as the vendor. Allow me to explain. Today when they sell a $200,000 license, they get 35 percent of the sales price, or $70,000. With $70,000, they can afford to pay the sales rep to drive the sales cycle and then perhaps make more money by doing the implementation of the software to the specific and unique requirements of the customer. Consider the same scenario in subscription view. Now the $200,000 might be spread over four years. That's $50,000 per year. Thirty-five percent of that number is now only $17,500—and the implementations are far more standard.

Indirect channels have been important to the software business, so it's no wonder people are trying to figure out what a next-generation channel will look like. Erin TenWolde and

Darren Bibby of IDC published a research paper[30] in late 2007.
Key highlights from their study were:

- There are still nascent partnering business models in the
  SaaS ecosystem. Based on interviews with SaaS
  providers, there is still a lot to learn and most of the
  activity is occurring on a trial-and-error basis.

- Traditional channel partners, particularly value-added
  resellers (VARs), have some potentially big challenges
  ahead, especially in terms of securing top-line revenue in
  resale scenarios. This will have implications on the
  valuations of VAR businesses, which traditionally have
  been valued based on a multiple of revenue.

- With many traditional IT challenges removed with SaaS,
  IDC believes those new solutions providers will emerge
  that are more business process oriented rather than
  technology focused. Those partners that can develop
  discrete expertise in niche areas will be well positioned
  to take advantage of the vast SaaS opportunity.

Axel Schultze, who founded Computer 2000, the largest
reseller of PCs in Europe, also founded a Model Six company
called Blueroads. He's uniquely positioned to discuss what a
next-generation channel might look like. Schultze remembers
1981, when IBM announced the PC, Compaq was founded, and
Microsoft introduced BASIC. He saw the first three to five
years of the PC industry focused on replacing existing midrange

---

[30] TenWolde, Erin and Bibby, Darren. The Emerging SaaS Channel. IDC Report #208547,
September 2007.

computers like IBM /34 or DEC PDP 11 with personal computers. This was a tough strategy and a cumbersome fight against established computer manufacturers, established software, established consulting processes and, most importantly, established sales channels.

Can we learn from the PC industry development in the 80's? What happened back then that led to the explosion of the PC industry and the enormous rise of companies like Compaq, IBM, Microsoft, Lotus, Ashton-Tate, and Intel? An interesting, almost unnoticed change happened: young startups entered the market and didn't sell into the established businesses, but into a new market segment—companies below $50M in revenue. They started selling in companies who never even wanted a large midrange or mainframe computer. And along those lines, a channel emerged that helped sell and install those PCs and PC software for $1000—a price a mid-size systems integrator wouldn't be bothered with. Axel boiled it down to a simple premise: "There is interesting software for a large variety of customers and industries. What is missing are the new channel companies." Will history repeat itself?

SHOW ME THE MONEY

You might have a killer application and a market that is
rapidly growing, but if you don't have money (and people) it
will be hard to turn it into a reality. This chapter focuses on the
money – some of the key metrics that you'll need to track in
order to insure a long running profitable business. We'll discuss
monthly recurring revenue (MRR), revenue recognition, churn,
the Magic Number and how much it takes to launch a new
business.

Revenue Recognition

Many traditional software companies are concerned about moving to Models Four through Six because of something called 'revenue recognition'. If a Model One company sells software for $1M, they recognize the million dollars on the day they sell it and it goes into the revenue for that quarter. If they were to sell that same system as software as a service, they may get $20,000 per month for the next 10 years. The same dollar amount is spent on applications, but logged in accounting books differently under Model Six. As a result, traditional (Model One) software companies have been concerned about experiencing a negative short-term impact on license revenue. This, of course, assumes that they choose to move to Model Five with their existing license business versus working in Model Four.

In the traditional software business, the largest part of revenues stems from vendors' license fees associated with software. A Model One company recognizes revenue from license fees when the software is shipped to the customer. Traditional software revenue accounting requires that the vendor's fee be allocated to the various elements based on something called vendor-specific objective evidence (VSOE). VSOE is limited to the price charged by the vendor for each element when it is sold separately. This requires the deferral of revenue until VSOE can be established for all elements in the arrangement or until all elements have been delivered. If customer support is the only undelivered element in the arrangement, however, the entire fee can be recognized ratably over the term of the customer support contract. In addition, recognition of revenue must be deferred if undelivered elements are essential to the functionality of any delivered elements.

Priscilla Morgan, former head of finance and business operations for Oracle On Demand says, "For those pursuing Model Four, the simplest way to think about providing software on demand is to treat the revenue the same as you have treated customer support." In fact, some of the same contractual terms and sales methodologies can be used. Contracts are yearly, subject to renewal by your support renewals teams. You'll also find out that your services will be much more specific than the terms you already have for product support. This way, one-time charges, such as implementations or customizations, can be treated the same way you have managed professional services contracts. In these cases, you'll have to recognize revenue based on milestones and the level of work that has been completed, but, once again, this should be no different than how this is done in your traditional software business.

Monthly Recurring Revenue (MRR)

Tien Tzuo, CEO of Zuora, points out that you're going to need the right metrics to run any Model Six business. A measure used by many Model Six companies is MRR (Monthly Recurring Revenue), which by the way, should also be used by Model One companies to track their support revenues.

MRR is a powerful idea but as such has both upside and downside. On the upside assume your company gets $50k of new MRR during your first twelve months of revenue generation. The rule of 78 says the company will generate a total of $3.9 million ($50k * 78) of revenue over that year. [Note: 78 is simply the total of the revenue months during the year; 12+11+10+...+1]. Furthermore – next year if it sells **no** new business revenue the company will still grow to $7.2M in year 2, since in the last month the company was doing $600K in MRR.

But what happens if the company does only $25k of MRR bookings. Now the first year revenue is only $1.95 million. And the company just missed its revenue number by $2 million. Worse yet, if your fixed operating costs are $600k per month, then the business is close to covering fixed operating expenses under the $50k MRR bookings scenario, but now 12 months away under the $25k MRR bookings scenario; assuming no churn. Meaning you'll need another $2M on cash/investment. Which of course brings us to the subject of cash.

Cash

As Subrah Iyer commented, Traditional Model One businesses have been great since with typical software license being sold for an Average Selling Price of say $500,000 could bring you the cash you needed to hire more people or buy more computers. Unfortunately, this is not exactly the case in a lower ASP, Model Six business model. However, if you could get a customer to change their payment terms and pay for the service a year in advance or better yet three years in advance it would do a lot to help your cash needs.

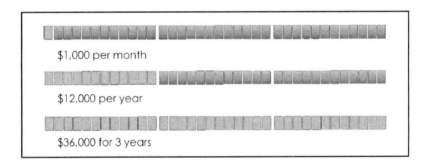

$1,000 per month

$12,000 per year

$36,000 for 3 years

Figure 9.1 Power of Payment Terms

Cost of Sales: When to Hire for More Sales

As we've repeated Model Six companies don't have the advantage of Model One companies, which historically have derived a large up front, license fee when a sale is completed. Moreover, the service requires significant infrastructure investment. "Every time we add an incremental customer, it costs us more money that quarter—it costs us more cash that quarter" explained Josh James, CEO of Omniture. To get a sense of the cost of service, Omniture operates a 15,000-server cloud for its 5,000 customers, and processes almost a trillion transactions per quarter. The financial consequences look exceptionally dire when expressed according to GAAP accounting rules, which force the cost to be expensed upfront. "When we were really stepping on the gas in 2004 we were GAAP unprofitable," said Josh. In 2005 Omniture's negative free cash flow was in excess of $22M—more than its total annual revenue—and it had spiked higher at some points. "It is a scary moment. Even when management understands the game plan and has the full support of its financial backers, it takes courage to plow ahead regardless," he said.

But when is it the time to step on the gas? When is it the time to ramp your sales force? Josh and Omniture have been relying on a simple calculation, shown is Figure 9.2 that produces what they call a Magic Number.

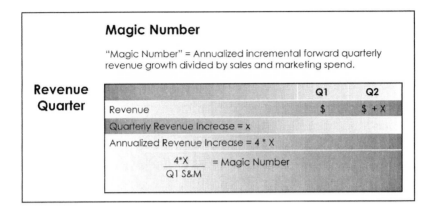

Figure 9.2 Magic Number Calculations

Figure 9.3 shows the analysis for a group of companies. According to the analysis any time the Magic Number is .75 or more, invest in more sales people and if the Magic Number is less than .5, there's probably something wrong with your business.

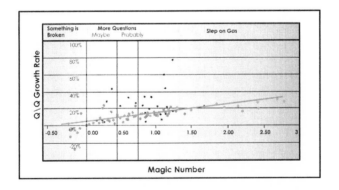

Figure 9.3 Magic Numbers for Model Six Companies

Churn: Cost of Keeping a Customer

Another critical metric for recurring businesses is churn, or its opposite, renewal. But there are many ways to calculate churn. For example, for any given period, what percent of the business at the start of the period is still there at the end of the period? The part that is lost is considered the churn. For companies with longer-term contracts, a renewal metric may be more appropriate. For a given period, such as a month, what percent of the business that is up for renewal actually renews?

Financial Systems

Many companies dramatically underestimate what it takes to run a Model Six business. In a Model One software company-- you express interest in purchasing my products, I write up an order form, ship you the products, send you an invoice, collect payment, and the transaction is completed.

Not so in the recurring revenue world. The first order is only the start of the relationship. Each month, I can measure how much of my service you are using and compute your bill. In addition, at any time, the customer may choose to change the service. Perhaps you have purchased a cell phone plan, and now you want to add text messaging. Perhaps you started off with 10 licenses of an application, and now want to add another 2 licenses. Or perhaps you subscribe to delivery of the New York Times, and you want to suspend delivery for 2 weeks while you are on vacation. Subscriptions are a living, breathing representation of the relationship between you and your clients, and every change to the subscription must be handled by all your back end systems from quoting, to billing, to order provisioning, and through to collections.

For any Model Six company, having the right billing and payment systems is important to growing and scaling the business. Any billing system, whether you buy or build must give you pricing and packaging flexibility. At Salesforce.com, Tien Tzuo, today CEO of Zuora, learned early on the importance of having the right pricing & packaging strategy in order to grow a subscription business. "When we first started, we thought the right strategy was to keep our pricing simple. We priced our sales force automation (SFA) service at $50 per user per month, and we thought that would be the price forever.

The market, though, had other ideas. Many tiny companies loved the idea of an on-demand service to manage their sales force, but they told us that $50 a person was too steep a price. At the other end of the spectrum, large companies like Autodesk told us they actually wanted to pay more -- but in return, they wanted more features, and stronger customer service.

We quickly realized that a one-size-fits-all pricing model would never work. Different companies had different needs, and different price points. That's when we embarked on our packaging strategy that ultimately led to a Professional Edition at $65 per person per month, an Enterprise Edition at $125 per person per month, and a Group Edition at $995 per year for 5 users."

If you look at other subscription companies like Netflix and Zipcar, you see the same evolution in their pricing models. Netflix started off in 2000 with a simple model -- $19.95/month. Fast-forward almost a decade, and Netflix now has over 9 plans hitting multiple price points. Their most popular plan is $16.99/month, labeled as the 3-DVD-at-a-time plan. But subscribers new to Netflix can dip their toe in the water with the $4.99/month 1-DVD-at-a-time plan, and heavy users can upgrade all the way to the 8-DVD-at-a-time plan for a whopping $47.99/month

Similar, Zipcar started off with a $50/year membership fee for their popular car sharing service. Today, Zipcar also has renamed the original plan as the "Occasional Driving Plan", and introduced 4 new price plans called "Extra Value Plans" for its heavy users. The basic lesson to learn here is that different customers have different needs. Customers want choice as to how they consume your services -- **and** how they pay – and the financial systems for service businesses need to reflect this degree of flexibility.

Financial Analysts

As a new company, you're going to hope that, one day; the financial analyst community will be talking about you. So what are they going to be interested in? How do they evaluate investments for the public markets?

Laura Lederman, a William Blair & Co. financial analyst who focuses on new software companies, sees three important evaluation criteria. The first thing she looks at is total available market. "It's the most important factor. The larger the market, the better the investment is likely to be." Number two on her list is the quality of management team. From her perspective, it's "one of the reasons Salesforce.com, Vocus, and Concur have all done so much better than other players in the market." And, finally, her third criterion is to evaluate the level of competition: the more competitive the market, typically the more difficult the investment.

Venture Capital

If you were a student of Salesforce.com and you'd know that it took $60M+ in capital to get the company to an IPO. This is also the same type of number in Webex's case. Of course the money was well spent since particularly in the later stage investments there was a direct correlation between investment in sales and revenue. Again, like WebEx, CRM took about six years to reach $100M in revenue. Students of traditional software companies know most of them struggle to get to $50M, and on a much slower growth curve. It is no wonder that both WebEx and Salesforce.com have high valuations relative to sales and earnings.

Salesforce.com (CRM)								
	1999	2000	2001	2002	2003	2004	2005	2006
Funding	$13M	$47M				IPO		
Subscription			$5,022	$21,513	$47,656	$85,796	$157,977	$280,639
Professional Service			$413	$896	$3,335	$10,227	$18,398	$29,218
Total Revenue			$5,435	$22,409	$50,991	$96,023	$176,375	$309,857
Cost of Subscription			$1,730	$3,718	$7,199	$7,782	$12,727	$34,457
Cost of Professional Service			$1,692	$2,329	$3,164	$9,491	$20,727	$34,669
Cost of Revenue			$3,422	$6,047	$10,363	$17,273	$33,454	$69,126
Gross Profit			$2,013	$16,362	$40,628	$78,750	$142,921	$240,731
Marketing & Sales			$25,392	$24,605	$33,522	$54,600	$96,311	$149,598
R&D			$3,366	$5,308	$4,648	$6,962	$9,822	$23,330
G&A			$6,855	$8,317	$12,958	$16,915	$30,268	$47,986
Lease Abandonment				$7,657		($3,455)		($285)
Total Operating Expense			$35,613	$45,887	$51,128	$75,022	$136,401	$220,629
Income			($33,600)	($29,525)	($10,500)	$3,728	$6,520	$20,102

Figure 9.4 Salesforce.com P&L

Ann Winblad began her career as a systems programmer, and in 1976, she co-founded Open Systems, Inc., an accounting software company, with a $500 investment. In 1998, she co-founded Hummer Winblad as the first venture capital firm to invest exclusively in software. Their first investment in a Model Six company was Employease in 1998. In a recent lecture at Stanford, Winblad discussed her view of software as a service, and identified a number of advantages. Having forward predictability, being independent of capital or IT budgets, being able to address unserved markets, and always "serving" the customer are all characteristics Winblad sees as being better.

Her key characteristics of a Model Six company are:

- Can be sold and delivered over the Web (via browser)
- Single instance, multi-tenant architecture
- Can be sold to small and medium size businesses (SMBs) as well as enterprises
- Requires little customization
- Requires low professional services
- Pricing model is subscription based (by time period, user or transactions)

Summary

Finance and business operations for a software product being delivered as an on-demand service are very different than what we're used to in the traditional software model. But if the sales, operations, and R&D can come together under a unified business model, the growth rates and valuations can be astonishing.

10

PEOPLE NEEDING PEOPLE

Software is a people business. Whether it's cloud computing, Web services, software as a service, or software on demand it makes no difference. In this chapter, we'll discuss some of the people challenges: finding or teaching the right skills, establishing the right organizations, and insuring you have the right people in the right jobs. If you're an existing software company, you'll face the Innovator's Dilemma. The challenge of growing a new business is difficult and getting the right team and the right model will be key. If you're a new software company, finding the right people and organizing them appropriately will be a constant challenge. But, all of this begins with people.

Economics

If we again use Webex as a case study of a successful company you can see in Figure 10.1 how the company's growth was tied to it's ability not only to raise money, but also to hire people, and lots of people.

1996	1997	1998	1999	2000	2001	2002	2003	2004
6	7	26	106	646	580	648	760	913

Figure 10.1 Hiring ramp at Webex

And by the way, not only to hire people, but also to fire people, as you can see in the year 2001. As a result much of the HR application cloud services have focused around recruiting (Taleo, Kenexa, etc.) and performance management (Successfactors, etc.).

Right People, Right Stage

For many of us, Geoffrey Moore's landmark book, *Crossing the Chasm*, best describes the lifecycle of a high tech company. In this and in subsequent books, Moore describes the seven major stages of a successful venture:

- Early Market – A time of great excitement when customers are technology enthusiasts and visionaries looking to be first to get on board with the new paradigm

- Chasm – A time of great despair, when the early-market's interest wanes but the mainstream market is still not comfortable with the immaturity of the solutions available

- Bowling Alley – a period of niche-based adoption in advance of the general marketplace, driven by compelling customer needs and the willingness of vendors to craft niche-specific whole products

- Tornado – a period of mass-market adoption, when the general marketplace switches over to the new infrastructure paradigm

- Main Street – a period of after-market development, when the base infrastructure has been deployed and the goal becomes to flesh out its potential

- Assimilation – the technology loses its discrete identity, moves into decline, and is supplanted by a new technology paradigm

While successful companies need to go through these stages, it's important to realize that people need to go through these stages as well. We often see that the CEO of a company at the early market stage is not the CEO of the company when it reaches Main Street. Of course, there are the rare exceptions of the individuals with the gift of being able to adapt, learn and change as they cross through each of these stages. Names like Jobs, Ellison, and Gates are the clear exceptions to the rule.

But for the rest of us, what are the characteristics that are most important in each of the stages? Tom Kippola, co-author of *The Gorilla Game*, recently said, "As a company is trying to cross the chasm, the title CEO does not mean Chief Executive Officer, instead it should mean Chief Experiment Officer." While, in hindsight, it might look like some companies took a straight line from inception to Fortune 500, the reality is, there were many left-turns, right-turns and U-turns along the way. Without the ability to quickly run experiments, learn from them, and then press on, most would have failed early in their lifecycle. Of course, there does come the day that experimentation and cheerleading need to be balanced with operational excellence. Making the quarterly sales numbers, delivering releases on time, and sticking to a budget are all requirements for any successful business. The mistake companies often make is putting an operationally excellent leader in place before they've crossed the chasm, or forgetting to get their operational house in order as they're headed down to Main Street. Getting the right people at the right stage, that's the ticket.

Right People

As with any team, having a good coach and quarterback is essential, but having the right people at all of the skill positions is the key to success. Delivering cloud services requires operational people, development people that are different from what we've seen in the traditional software world.

As Evan Goldberg pointed out, your engineering group needs to both have a "high tolerance for change" as well as be "accurate and careful programmers." Furthermore, you're going to need what he calls next generation DBAs, operations people who understand both software development and software delivery. Lynn Reedy recommends you have the VP of R&D work for the VP of Operations; or vice versa. By doing so, it forces conflicts between the race for new features and the ability to manage change in a reliable way. Clearly, this is something we never had to do in traditional software companies.

So, where are you going to find these skilled people? One place to look is in the traditional software product support organizations. People who have had to optimize performance or availability of software implementations in the field will have been exposed to some of the key processes and challenges involved with delivering Web applications. Often times, these individuals are leading premium support services and are located at or near a customer site. The challenge for these people is that their tendency will be to customize a solution for each customer installation. You'll have to find the people that can generalize the lessons learned in the field and apply them in a standard, uniform way.

You may also discover some of the greatest expertise to be individuals who have been in end-user operations where they have had to manage applications for a large internal population (e.g., the people who ran American Airlines SABRE). Many of these people have run large-scale operations. Rick Dalzell, who recently retired from Amazon and was their Senior Vice President of Operations and CIO, was recruited out of Wal-Mart.

Culture

In 1998, 24-year-old Tony Hsieh sold his company, Internet advertiser LinkExchange, to Microsoft for $265M. What some people don't know is he sold it because he stopped wanting to come into work. While LinkExchange had been a successful company, he never focused on the company culture, the common values shared by everyone in a group. So it should be no surprise that when he invested in and later became CEO of Zappos, the leading online shoe retailer he made culture a cornerstone of the company. Culture starts from the hiring process, where they ask, "Which superhero would you want to be?" and continues thru their four weeks of training where every employee (even VPs) answers phones in the call center and ships shoes out of their distribution facility in Kentucky.

After the training, they are offered $2,000 to leave the company—no questions asked. This "quit now" bonus, which started at $100, is designed to ensure employees are there for the right reasons. In 2008 less than 1% of the trainees accept what the company calls "the offer."

Zappos.com also publishes a "Culture Book" every year. It's several hundred pages of employees from all across the company describing what the company culture means to them. The company itself maintains 10 core values:

1. Deliver WOW through service
2. Embrace and drive change
3. Create fun and a little weirdness
4. Be adventurous, creative, and open-minded
5. Pursue growth and learning
6. Build open and honest relationships with communication
7. Build a positive team and family spirit
8. Do more with less
9. Be passionate and determined
10. Be humble

Tony says, "Our number one focus is our company culture." For Zappos.com, a great culture translates into great service. "We want people who are passionate about what Zappos is about - service. I don't care if they're passionate about shoes." This passion has translated to hundreds of stories of how Zappos employees have delivered unexpected service, including finding out a place to get food, when the hotel had closed room service.

Scrape

For those that are attempting to transform existing Model One software companies there are many unique challenges. You have three fundamental organizational approaches. We'll call these Scrape, Buy New and Remodel. Scrape refers to an "all-in" approach to moving from Model One to Model Six. Buy New means to acquire companies with Model Six business models and Remodel refers to adopting a Model Four or Model Five business in parallel with your traditional Model One business.

The Scrape strategy is best illustrated by Concur. Concur is a unique case study—a company that made the transition from a traditional license model to software as a service: from Model One to Model Six as a publicly traded company. Figure 10.2 shows you the transformation in revenue terms. You can see the license revenue line marching to zero, along with the growth of the subscription line. If you were to look at the stock price for

Concur when CEO Steve Singh made the announcement that they would shift business models, you'd see the price crashing below $1 a share, so this is not a change that's easy to make. CEO Steve Singh says Concur was able to do this because the 2001 Internet Bubble burst gave them an environment where no one wanted to own technology stocks. Of course, with the global meltdown of 2008, maybe we are entering another window of opportunity.

Concur (CNQR)							
	2000	2001	2002	2003	2004	2005	2006
Subscription	$927	$4,624	$10,360	$33,590	$40,244	$53,011	$80,501
License	$14,852	$12,489	$9,847	$8,690	$4,746	$2,617	$0
Professional Service	$2,282	$23,771	$24,890	$14,457	$11,560	$16,203	$16,644
Total Revenue	$38,604	$40,884	$45,097	$56,737	$56,550	$71,831	$97,145
Cost of License	$1,342	$584	$487				
Cost of Subscription	$2,806	$8,615	$9,957				
Cost of Service	$23,684	$15,762	$11,543				
Gross Profit	$27,832	$24,961	$21,987	$23,214	$23,264	$28,450	$37,846
Marketing & Sales	$38,581	$24,941	$16,669	$14,549	$14,329	$17,484	$22,907
R&D	$31,212	$16,449	$10,606	$10,356	$8,773	$9,336	$12,445
G&A	$14,795	$10,729	$6,800	$46,710	$7,295	$10,319	$14,458
Acq & Restruct	$2,167	$266	$1,490	$1,140	$1,140	$1,140	$2,420
Total Operating Expense	$114,587	$77,346	$57,552	$55,969	$54,801	$66,729	$90,076
Income	-$75,983	-$36,462	-$12,455	$768	$1,749	$5,102	$7,069

Figure 10.2 Concur P&L

The Scrape strategy can work, but the transition will not be easy. During the shift, Concur went from 700 employees to 300 and replaced the majority of the executive team. Not something for the faint of heart.

Buy New

Buying a Model Six company is another strategy a Model One company can adopt. In this strategy you'll be best served by purchasing companies with products in adjacent markets, or in with products that sell to customers significantly smaller than your current customer base. Once acquired you'll need to be cautious of the "white corpuscles", which will organizationally seek to envelop the foreign group and in time destroy it. Your challenge will be to leverage the knowledge of the people in development and delivery of the applications as well as in the new techniques for marketing and sales. Give them the opportunity to teach and share their experiences. Consider making their VP of Operations responsible for operations of the entire company, or make the same step in sales or marketing.

Perhaps the most famous example is Siebel's acquisition of UpShot. In the late 90s UpShot was in head-to-head competition with Salesforce.com, as anyone traveling through the San Francisco airport would have seen. Those of you considering the acquisition strategy might consider the story of UpShot as told by founder Keith Raffel. These days, Raffel has become an author of a different kind, having just released his second novel *Smasher*, a popular mystery set in Palo Alto.[31]

---

[31] Raffel, Keith. *Smasher.* Midnight Ink, 2008.

In the early 1990s, Raffel was working at a start-up where there was no good way to send leads out to the field sales team. Not only that, but when the CEO asked him how effective the marketing programs were, he would point to all the deals that could be traced to one campaign or another. The salespeople would then pipe up and claim that they already knew about any prospect the marketing team uncovered. So Raffel came up with a way to distribute leads and send them out to the field using email and an electronic bulletin board (remember them?).

When Keith saw the first Netscape browser in 1994, the light bulb went on. Raffel took a leave of absence and started working on a prototype in 1995, and founded UpShot in 1996. Their aim was to make traditional CRM tools more accessible and affordable by using the Web. Raffel started by finding what he calls "a brilliant engineer, who was between gigs" to build a prototype. He showed the prototype to ten companies, and nine said they would buy it. So he built a team that included Kris Olson to lead marketing and Bob Schulman as head of engineering, and proceeded to rent space above a Jaguar dealer in Redwood City. As Olson said, "HP might have been founded in a garage, but UpShot was founded over one." Raffel tells a story from the early days and gives you a glimpse into the role of a start-up CEO. "A key engineer came to me one day and said that the paint fumes from below were leaking into his office. I went to the hardware store, bought some Spackle, and patched the walls."

UpShot became the first CRM software delivered as a service in August 1999, about the time Salesforce.com was founded. They signed up Fortune 500 companies like Johnson & Johnson, Xerox, and HP. But ultimately they needed more money to fuel the sales and marketing engine (remember what we talked about in the last chapter). So, in 2003, they sold Upshot to Siebel. From that point on, unfortunately, momentum slowed. Revenue for the UpShot product, as we know, is recognized over time and therefore, unfortunately, Siebel salespeople received their commissions stretched out over time. It took a year to fix this problem.

In addition, at the time of the acquisition, Siebel was ready to launch an internal Model Six product, which was not as fully featured as UpShot. Nevertheless, Siebel went with what they had developed internally. More momentum was lost. And finally, a big New York investment bank wanted to purchase a huge number of seats of the Siebel Model Six offering and asked for new features. The decision to accommodate them, made against the advice of the UpShot team, took them even further off course, and still more momentum was lost. While things improved gradually, everything changed again when Siebel was purchased by Oracle in 2006. As Raffel says, "That chapter is being written by others. So it goes in Silicon Valley."

Remodel

Finally, Model One companies have the opportunity to create Model Four or Five businesses to run in parallel with their traditional business. While we've discussed the advantages of doing this, let's focus on the organizational challenges you'll have. First, there will be conflict on the delivery side with any premium support offerings or professional services offerings your company is providing. These teams will say a standardized Model Four or Model Five service offering is too restrictive and worse yet will often block access to the customer. By the way, a well constructed Model Four service will be lower cost, which will threaten them even more. Finally, these new services will not endear you to any of your channel partners, who not only resell your software, but also provide a box and a body. Your challenge will be to find was at worse to neutralize them, at best to create new opportunities to package your service as part of a larger offering. This brings us to sales.

Your biggest advantage in the Remodel strategy is that you can leverage the existing sales force. An application sales person can either double the size of the deal (application license plus first year of the service), or competitively out position other traditional software providers. Probably one of the best stories from the Oracle On Demand experience was competing head to head with SAP for an enterprise application sale to the largest mining company in Latin America. Oracle did not look to have any advantage, as SAP was both stronger in Latin America and stronger in mining as a vertical market. But Luis Meisler, EVP of Latin America, and Alberto Chacin, VP for Oracle On Demand in Latin America, devised a strategy that won the business. How?

In a meeting with the mining company CIO we said, "In the end, an SAP or Oracle application purchase price will be nearly the same, probably somewhere near a million dollars." The CIO agreed. "What have you budgeted to manage the application?" We were guessing it was about $4M a year, based on the rule of thumb that the cost to manage the software is four times the purchase price. The CIO answered $6M per year. So we said, "In that case, over five years the cost of this application, whether from SAP or Oracle will cost you $31M: $1M to purchase the software and $30M to manage the software. So, you can buy the software from SAP and manage it yourself or you can buy the software from Oracle and manage it yourself. In either case it will be $31M. However, there is a third alternative: let Oracle manage the software for $15M."

The Oracle sales person assigned to the mining company not only won the business from SAP but also received a significantly higher compensation, given that the deal included the license as well as the first year of the services. So you can see, once your application sales force is compensated for selling On Demand, you will quickly bring them into alignment with your goals. Organizationally, you'll have to create an on-demand sales overlay team and focus on delivering a lot of information about how this solution is simpler, cheaper, and better than doing it the old-fashioned way. Once you have that core group of reference customers, you'll be ready to 'cross the chasm'.

World of Work

So how much will our work lives change in the future? What will be the nature of work? Here there are lessons to be learned from the world of online gaming. *World of Warcraft*, an elaborate fantasy computer game, is part of a growing number of MMORPGs (Massively Multi-player Online Role Playing Games).   With over seven million subscribers, at any moment in time, there are hundreds of thousands, if not a million, people simultaneously playing the game. What are they doing? While some are merely spectators, the vast majority are working with other people—people they know, people they don't, some old, some young, in Beijing, in London—all to achieve an objective. Sounds like the modern World of Work, doesn't it?

So, how is it that *World of Warcraft* accomplishes something that we find so difficult in the world of work? One of the keys to the success of *World of Warcraft* is the idea that an individual's skills are known and non-overlapping. Some characters have the ability to kill, but not heal. And other characters can heal, but cannot slay.

Our business world needs to extend these fundamental ideas in software that brings information and people into a network. Consider the latest Boeing aircraft, the 787 Dreamliner. The company has pushed outsourcing of component parts to new levels. In the 787, outside suppliers are responsible for about 70 percent of the aircraft parts, versus a previous mark of 50 percent. These suppliers span the globe as shown below.

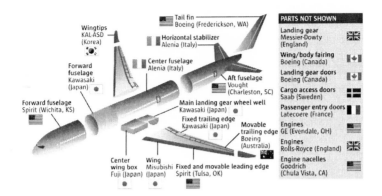

Figure 10.3 The World is Flat

The world might be flat, but our software isn't. Business managers can no longer 'manage by walking around', like the great David Packard taught a generation of HP managers to do. Today we're all doing conference calls at 4:00 in the afternoon, because it's the best time for Asia, Europe, and North America to talk. If you want to read an entire book on the implications of games check out the new book[32] by Byron Reeves and J. Leighton Read.

Summary

Early in 2007, Abhijit Dubey of McKinsey & Co. led a team that surveyed CIOs regarding the SaaS model. They learned that the proportion of CIOs considering adopting application cloud

---

[32] Byron Reeves and J. Leighton Read: Games at Work: How Games and Virtual Worlds Are Changing the Way People Work and Businesses Compete.

services in the coming year has grown from 38 percent the previous year to 61 percent in 2007. Dubey and Dilip Wagle, a partner at McKinsey's Seattle office, have published a report entitled *"Delivering Software as a Service."* There are many interesting comments in the report, but perhaps the best quote is: "And finally, they'll have to build the management processes and organizational structures to manage two distinct but potentially mutually cannibalizing businesses (traditional software and software as a service) with different business models and requiring remarkably different sets of capabilities. Although this challenge is formidable, software executives who continue to put it off risk being left behind."

We could not agree more.

11

BEGINNING OF SOFTWARE

Congratulations on making it to the end of the book. Hopefully, you've found it enlightening and entertaining, and you'll repeat some of the campfire stories. If, as some people believe, this is the third wave of computing, following mainframes and client-server then we are indeed at the beginning of another generation of software as revolutionary as Excel, Word, Powerpoint, SAP Financial applications and Oracle databases were in the last generation.

This software can take advantage of 1000s of computers, near infinite storage and a network of mobile eyes and ears that number in the billions.

For those of you in the traditional software business model, you have many choices. Do you attempt to build a Model Four business? Do you acquire a Model Six business, or do three of your colleagues leave and start a new venture using your specialized expertise? For those of you already in a Model Six business, perhaps the book has given you a better understanding of the challenges your fellow team members face, and you're starting to think about how information and community will change your business in the future.

A few years ago, the CEO of a company that builds sales compensation software in the traditional model asked me if he should deliver his software as a service. Of course, I told him all of the good reasons he should consider doing it. Time passed, and he called me again and said he'd made the decision and now that he was well on his way, he asked me what he should think about next. I told him it has to become more about the information and less about the software. He said, "Interesting, most of my customers are starting to ask me—what is the best sales comp plan?"

Now most of us in the software business are used to being asked for more features and functions, but here the customers are asking for something even more valuable: knowledge, information. Perhaps this is why few of us see Amazon, eBay or Google as software companies, because what we see when we when we use their applications is the *information*: the Pez dispenser, the best seller, the top 10 places to stay in Tahiti.

We already have pointed out that consumer Internet applications are all content rich. All of you who are running software as a cloud service are sitting on valuable business knowledge. Concur today processes over 10 percent of the expense reports in the U.S. The information about what hotels, which airlines, and what times of the year travel is happening is far more valuable than the transactional efficiency afforded by delivering expense management as a service. Taleo's systems have seen millions of resumes. What is the value of knowing where there is a deficit in skills, by geography? What if an on-demand CRM software vendor were to analyze all of the configured workflows and identify patterns of sales processes with the shortest sales closing periods? Again, what VP of Sales would not pay to know what sales processes are the most efficient in a particular industry or geography? Few people may realize this, but to assess the overall health of the economy, the United States' government contracts with Visa and MasterCard to understand aggregated data of how much each of us, as a consumer, spends. Again, the value of the information far outweighs the value of the credit card transaction processing.

Of course, such usage of customer data remains a controversial topic, as many will be nervous about their trade secrets being published as best practices. Publication and resale of identifiable private data obviously violates legal regulations and privacy laws. But, what rules apply to aggregated information? When you log on to Amazon, you're contributing to their overall knowledge of consumer interests with every click. Why isn't this the case for business software?

We could go on and on with new companies and ideas, but hopefully you get the point. Software is far from a mature industry. We're much closer to the Beginning of Software, or what some call the "Golden Age of Software." We hope this book has given you some insights into how to think about the future of your business, whether you're part of a large software company or three people with a great idea in Olathe, Kansas.

INDEX

T

U

V

W

X

Y

INDEX